DISCOVER CORK

Praise for the *City Guides* series

'Whether you're a visitor from abroad, or you're
just interested in finding out more about your
native land, these informative
City Guides are well worth reading'

The Sunday Tribune

KIERAN McCARTHY is a born and bred Corkonian. He graduated from UCC in 1999 with a BA degree in Geography and Archaeology. He has lectured and researched widely on Cork's history in association with numerous institutions, including UCC, Cork Institute of Technology, the Cork Education and Support Centre, and the Vocational Educational Committee. In April 2002, Kieran co-ordinated the successful *Lord Mayor's Schools' History Project*, and in 2003 co-ordinated his own *Discover Cork: Schools' History Project*. He has been involved in the compilation of several television reports on Cork, the most recent in 2001 for RTÉ's *Nationwide*. Kieran writes a weekly column in *Inside Cork*, and has published two books, *Pathways Through Time, Historical Walking Trails of Cork City* and *Cork: A Pictorial Journey*. Kieran currently works as a freelance historical consultant and is pursuing a M.Phil in UCC. For further information on Kieran's work, see www.obrien.ie

ACKNOWLEDGEMENTS

A book such as this cannot be penned without the support of numerous individuals. First and foremost I would like to thank Michael O'Brien, Rachel Pierce and Emma Byrne of The O'Brien Press for their professionalism throughout this project. I would like to acknowledge the staff of the Cork city and county libraries and also the staff of the Boole Library, UCC. Thanks also to the management of Cork City Council, Cork Institute of Technology, UCC; Cork–Kerry Tourism and Cork City Tourism. Appreciation is also due to Peter Murray and the staff of the Crawford Municipal Art Gallery, Stella Cherry of Cork Public Museum, Tony O'Connell, Anne Kearney and *Irish Examiner Publications* and Claire Flahavan for permission to publish a section of her depiction of Viking Cork. I would like to acknowledge the support of the Committee of Cork as European City of Culture 2005. Thanks are also due to Eddie Lyons, Editor of *Inside Cork*, and his staff for their support. In addition, references for the material in this book can be found in the author's weekly historical column in *Inside Cork* (October 1999–time of writing). Finally, sincere thanks to my family and friends for their consistent support and encouragement.

DISCOVER
CORK

KIERAN McCARTHY

THE O'BRIEN PRESS
DUBLIN

DEDICATION

For my friends – for their encouragement,

support and for never asking why

First published 2003 by The O'Brien Press Ltd,
20 Victoria Road, Dublin 6, Ireland.
Tel: +353 1 4923333; Fax: +353 1 4922777
E-mail: books@obrien.ie
Website: www.obrien.ie

ISBN: 0-86278-817-X

British Library Cataloguing-in-Publication Data
McCarthy, Kieran
Discover Cork. - (O'Brien city guides series)
1.Cork (Ireland) - Guidebooks
2.Cork (Ireland) - History
I.Title
914.1'956'04824

1 2 3 4 5 6 7 8 9 10
03 04 05 06 07

Editing, typesetting, layout and design: The O'Brien Press Ltd
Modern map of Cork: Design Image
Printing: GraphyCEMS

PICTURE CREDITS
The author and publisher wish to thank the following for permission to reproduce images:
Courtesy of the Crawford Municipal Art Gallery: front cover (top), back cover, pp. 41, 124,
126 (both), 127 and Colour Section: pp. 11 (top), 12; Claire Flahavan: extract from map,
p.12; Courtesy of Cork Public Museum: pp. 10, 23, 24, 27, 44, 51, 52, 55 and Colour Section:
p. 3 (top); Courtesy of *The Irish Examiner*: pp. 18, 58, 67, 110; *Illustrated London News*: pp.
101, 112; Courtesy of Cork City Library: pp. 21, 26, 37, 71, 78; Emma Byrne: front cover
(top), back cover, pp. 59, 60, 61, 72, 108, 113, 124, 126 (both), 127 and Colour Section: pp.
9, 10 (both), 11 (both), 12, 13 (both), 14, 16 (bottom); Courtesy of Tony O'Connell
Photography: pp. 63, 88 and Colour Section: pp. 1 (bottom), 2, 4 (top and bottom), 5, 6
(bottom), 7 (both), 8, 15 (both), 16 (top); Kieran McCarthy: front cover (middle and
bottom), pp. 8, 13, 15, 16, 29, 31, 32, 34, 39, 43, 46, 48, 49, 70, 73, 75, 81, 85, 89, 92, 94, 95,
98, 104, 115, 117, 118, 121 and Colour Section: pp. 1 (top), 3 (bottom), 6 (top).
While every effort has been made to contact copyright-holders, if any error or omission has
occurred the copyright-holder should contact the publisher.
Valerie Fleury of Discover Cork Guided Tours has consented to the use of *Discover Cork* as
the title of this book.

CONTENTS

PART ONE: THE HISTORY OF THE CITY

PART TWO: GUIDE TO THE HISTORIC CITY

THE HISTORY OF THE CITY

Discover Cork

'... leaving us, the summer visitor says in his
good-humoured way that Cork is quite a busy place
... as humdrum a collection of odds and ends as ever
went by the name of city – are flung higgledy piggledy
together into a narrow double-streamed, many
bridged river valley, jostled and jostling, so compacted that the mass throws up a froth and flurry that
confuses the stray visitor ... for him this is Cork.'

Daniel Corkery's account in *The Threshold of Quiet* (1917) provides a
good description of the physical landscape of Cork. The mixed
'collection of odds and ends' reflects the manner of the city's evolution. It was built by a combination of native and outside influences,
its ever-changing townscape and society shaped by different cultures
since its origin as a monastic settlement. The city possesses a distinct character, derived from a mixture of its plan, topography, buildings and location.

Cork is unique among Irish cities in that it alone has experienced
every phase of Irish urban development from c.AD600 to the present
day. The settlement at Cork began as a monastic centre in the seventh century, founded by St FinBarre. It served as a Viking port
before the Anglo-Normans arrived and created a prosperous walled
town; it grew through the influx of English colonists during the sixteenth and seventeenth centuries and suffered the political problems
inherent in Irish society at that time; it was altered significantly in
Georgian and Victorian times when reclamation of its marshes
became a priority, along with the construction of spacious streets
and grand town houses; its quays, docks and warehouses exhibit the
impact of the industrial revolution; and in the last 100 years,
Corkonians have witnessed both the growth of extensive suburbs and
the rejuvenation of the inner city. Built on the valleysides of the
River Lee, the city's suburbs are the result of a spiralling population
in the twentieth century.

Perhaps the most important influence on the city's development
was and is the River Lee, which has witnessed the evolution of the city
from monastic centre to cosmopolitan twenty-first-century city.
Originally, Cork comprised a series of marshy islands, reflected in

A view of Cork, with its famous quays and bridge

the Irish name for the city, Corcaigh, or 'marshes'. Just west of the city centre the Lee splits into two channels, each flowing around the city before meeting again in Cork harbour. This means the city centre is an island, bounded by the North River and the South River. The urban centre was built on the lowest crossing-point of the Lee, where it meets the sea. This situation has given the city a rich maritime history and a strong identification as a port town.

Alongside the city's physical development is the story of its people. In character they are astute, confident and often rebellious – a trait passed down through generations and remembered in Cork songs and oral tradition. Corkonians make Cork unique. A walk through St Patrick's Street, affectionately known as 'Pana', confirms the warmth of its people, the rich accent, the hustle and bustle of a great city.

St FinBarre – the Man and the Myth

The foundation of the city has been attributed to an Early Christian monk named FinBarre, now the patron saint of Cork. It is thought he was born around AD560 near Garranes, County Cork. Folklore relates that FinBarre (*Fionn-barra*, or fair-headed one) was educated as a monk and established several churches in the Munster area. One of these sites was located on a rocky island in the centre of a lake over-looked by the Shehy Mountains, where the River Lee rises. The name of this lake today is Gougane Barra, or 'FinBarre's rocky place'.

There is not much information on the layout of this early monas-tery. In 1750 eminent antiquary and historian Charles Smith noted that the remains of a stone wall were present on the site. This wall would have enclosed stone-built or timber cells, a church and other domestic buildings. Based on this account and other partial remains, a replica of this monastery was constructed at the site in the nine-teenth century. A large wooden cross is said to mark the spot occu-pied by FinBarre's own cell.

As a result of his piety and good works, FinBarre's reputation spread and his once quiet island hermitage became a place of pil-grimage. Seeking solitude, FinBarre left to find a place for a new her-mitage. Bounded on all sides by the Shehy Mountains, FinBarre followed the easiest route out of the area: the River Lee. His search led him to walk the full length of the river from its source to its mouth, a distance of approximately seventy kilometres. It was at this point, the mouth of the river, that he chose to set up a small hermit-age on the southern valleyside. FinBarre was granted land by a local chieftain named Hugh Uí Meic Iar. The name of the area was Corcach Mór na Mumhan, or the Great Marsh of Munster. Today, it is occu-pied by the commercial heart of Cork City centre.

FinBarre's hermitage was located around the area of present-day Gillabbey Street. It grew to be an important religious centre and soon it became necessary to expand the site. Between AD600 and AD800, a larger hermitage was constructed east of the original site on open ground now marked by St FinBarre's Cathedral. It is believed that over the subsequent centuries this hermitage grew to a point where it extended along the northern district of the Lough, and extended on both sides of Gillabbey Street and College Road about as far as the locality now occupied by University College Cork (UCC).

Around the year AD623, St FinBarre died at the monastery of his friend, St Colmán, at Cloyne in east Cork. His body was returned to his hermitage and his remains were encased in a silver shrine. Here they remained until 1089 when they were stolen by Dermod O'Brien. The shrine and the remains have never been recovered. Legend has it that the location of his tomb is just to the southeast of the present cathedral, overlooked by the famous Golden Angel.

During the reconstruction of the cathedral in the 1860s, renowned Cork antiquary Richard Caulfield found several items of interest. Caulfield describes that at the northeast corner of the new cathedral, the underlining limestone rock dipped and it was therefore necessary to dig down approximately ten metres to establish proper foundations near the bedrock – a depth that bordered on the water basin of the River Lee. It was here that a burial place was revealed, containing several human craniums. When the foundations were being laid in the southeast corner in August 1865, Caulfield's dig

St FinBarre, patron saint of Co

revealed a large trough-like object. This proved to be an ablutonium, a trough used for washing one's hands and feet before entering a church. As St FinBarre's tomb is said to be located in this corner of the cathedral, some believe the ablutonium could be a marker indicating the position of the saint's last resting place.

Raiders from the Sea

Between the seventh and ninth centuries, the monastery overlooking Corcach Mór na Mumhan flourished financially, as did many other monasteries in Ireland and in Britain. Most enjoyed a steady income, and gold and silver were donated by patrons and were used in the manufacture of religious objects, such as chalices and crosses. Their peace and prosperity was soon to be threatened, however.

The first wave of invaders came from Norway and became known as Northmen or Vikings, a name originating from the Norwegian word *vikingr*, meaning pirate or raider. All that is known of the first recorded attack on the monastery at Corcach Mór na Mumhan was that it occurred in AD820 and the most valuable treasures were plundered. It is also known that it was raided four to five times in the ensuing 100 years.

It was during this period that monasteries first built defensive buildings. The construction of a tall round tower with a doorway placed high above the ground provided a safe house for all valuable goods and manuscripts. The monastery in Cork had such a round tower, which would have been located just east of the present-day St FinBarre's Cathedral, the site of which is now overlooked by the Golden Angel. The tower was intact up to the mid-eighteenth century, after which it began to deteriorate rapidly, leaving no remains.

Upon landing at Corcach Mór na Mumhan, the Vikings were met by an area that differed markedly from the city we know today. No physical features of the present-day city centre existed around AD800. At that time, the area was basically a small-scale delta – a marshland with a series of alluvial or sandy islands dotted along its length. The River Lee wound its way between the islands, meandering through a valley dominated by two steep and heavily forested valleysides to the north and the south. At high tide these islands were invisible, reappearing again at low tide. On these marshy islands there would have been an abundance of rushes and reeds carpeting the ground.

The environment would not have been entirely welcoming, but the Norwegians nonetheless established a settlement, or *longphort*, here. We cannot be sure of the exact location of the Viking town, but it is known that in AD848 a settlement base called Dún Corcaighe, or Fort of the Marshes, was besieged by Olchobar, King of Caiseal in North Munster. The settlement at Cork was probably surrounded by a stockade, encompassing a crowded town with numerous timber dwellings aligning a central street, which would have doubled as a trading area. It is thought that it was located on an island, the core of which could be marked by South Main Street, an area that was developed in ensuing centuries by other colonists. The Norwegians established a maritime network with other Viking ports, namely those at Dublin, Waterford, Wexford and Limerick.

The presence of the Vikings was not tolerated kindly by the Native Irish and there was intermittent conflict between the two groups. The coastal aspect of the Viking settlements was no coincidence. Inland, Gaelic clans would have outnumbered the Vikings. While they did conduct incursions into the interior by use of the river system, they established bases only in port areas, where escape by boat could be swift, if necessary.

Viking Settlement and Society

The Norwegian presence in Corcach Mór na Mumhan was interrupted by invaders from Denmark c.AD914. In Cork, these new invaders – the Danish Vikings – started by raiding the monastery on the hillside, but

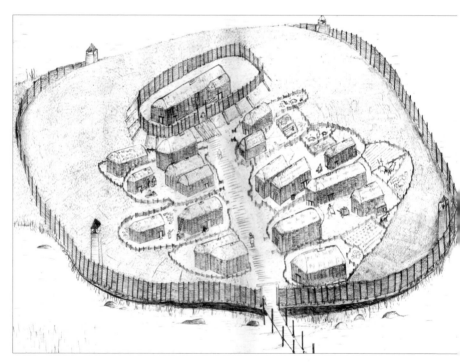

Reconstruction of the Viking island settlement at Corcach Mór na Mumhan, the area of which is now marked by Beamish and Crawford Brewery

soon turned their attention to wealthier and more powerful king-
doms in Munster.

The Danes decided to settle in Ireland. They took over and adapted
existing Norwegian bases and constructed additional ones to a similar but larger design. Unfortunately, there is little information available regarding a Danish settlement at Cork, but there are some clues
that give an insight into the location, structure and society of Danish
Viking Age Cork. It is known that there were at least three main areas
of settlement.

The first area of settlement was located south of FinBarre's monastery, on a hillside, extending from what is now French
Quay–Barrack Street to the area of George's Quay. In 1989 excavations at no.2 French Quay
revealed six timber posts, which
were once part of a small Danish
Viking dock. From the few historical records available, it is
known that this settlement was
bounded by the monastery on
one side and by a cross called
Carmelaire on the other. On the
other side there was a little harbour, reflected in the current
name Cove Street, and a central
routeway that led to St Sepulchre's Church, located in the
area of present-day Douglas
Street. In fact, St Sepulchre's is
alleged to be one of four Christian churches founded in Late
Viking Age Cork, c.AD1000. The
other four included St Mary del
Nard and St Michael's, both
located just west of present-day
Barrack Street, St Brigid's,
located in the present-day area of
Deerpark, in Turner's Cross, and
St John the Evangelist, located

Evidence of the Viking inhabitation of Cork exists in
the form of the placename Keyser's Hill (*above*),
meaning 'the path leading to the quayside'.

somewhere in what is now the central campus of UCC.

The second habitation zone was located on an adjacent marshy island, an area now occupied by the brewery of Beamish and Crawford, South Main Street, Hanover Street and Bishop Lucey Park. A fortification of either timber or stone encompassed the settlement, and the entrance comprised a timber bridge called Droichet, similar to the Irish derivation *droichead*, meaning 'bridge'. In Viking times Droichet would have linked the second Viking habitation zone on the island to the first habitation zone on the southern hillside. South Gate Bridge now marks the spot of Droichet.

Since 1977 there have been several archaeological excavations in the South Main Street area which have revealed Danish Viking Age material. Among the most prominent of these finds are: a trackway and oyster-shell pits, discovered on the site of Bishop Lucey Park; foundations, a hearth and roof supports of a mid-twelfth-century sill-beam house found off Hanover Street, plus broken pottery sherds; part of an early twelfth-century timber property fence revealed when foundations were being laid for a nightclub on Tuckey Street. Work by the Cork Main Drainage Scheme on the intersection of Washington Street and South Main Street uncovered part of a Late Viking Age wattle house.

The third habitation zone was situated on the northern valleyside, primarily around present-day lower Blackpool, through which the Kiln River flows before joining the northern channel of the River Lee. In the 1920s, work on John Street revealed a stone with the inscription: St John's Mill AD1020, indicating the presence of a watermill on the Kiln River. In 1844, just north of this site at Kilbarry in upper Blackpool, a Viking Age hoard was discovered, comprising approximately fifty silver rings in a wooden box.

It is known that trading took place in the Danish Viking settlement. Goods such as wine (for church use) and salt (for preserving meat) were the main commodities imported. The exact source of these imports is unknown; documentary evidence suggests that the trading network reached across to Britain and France. In terms of exports, it is likely that the principle exports were sheeps' wool, fish and hides and meat from cattle.

We also know that trade was conducted with the monastery and with local Gaelic families, with whom the Vikings had made alliances. Adjacent to the Viking settlement on the northern valleyside was a ringfort settlement called Sean Dún (later anglicised as Shandon). Sean Dún, which means 'old fort', was one of a number of fortifications owned by the McCarthy clan in Cork and Kerry.

To obtain an overview of what the Viking settlement may have been like for its citizens, we must combine information from finds in Cork with evidence retrieved at excavations in Waterford and Dublin. The settlement on the island had a central routeway on a north–south axis. Property plots, laneways, outhouses and storage pits would have run at right angles to the routeway itself. Houses within the settlement would have been small and basic, comprising one large room and a maximum of two other rooms. They would have been made of timber or wattle-and-daub with thatched roofs. Life in the town would have been difficult due to overcrowding, inadequate waste disposal and the effects of living on damp, marshy land. Infectious diseases such as influenza and tuberculosis would have been rife.

Early Anglo-Norman Settlement and Society

The power-sharing agreement between the Vikings and the McCarthy clan was opposed and changed by the Anglo-Normans, who arrived at Bannow Bay on the coast of Wexford in 1169, led by Richard de Clare, better known as Strongbow. They came at the invitation of power-

View across to the brewery of Beamish and Crawford, formerly the site of the Viking island settlement and the early Anglo-Norman walled town.

St Nicholas Church, built as a symbol of the Anglo-Norman victory over the Danes and Native Irish.

hungry Diarmuid MacMurrough, an Irish chieftain who wished to be High King and saw this foreign force as a means of achieving his ambition. The Anglo-Normans quickly established themselves as the dominant force, subduing several Gaelic and Viking groups on the east coast. King Henry II, realising the fiscal benefits Ireland could afford the Crown, sent a large force to colonise other urban areas. The Normans reorganised the towns under their control as manorial societies, that is, a society in which land and lordship are of central importance and are supported by the creation of clustered settlements. These towns were to function primarily as market places for the produce of the manor and surrounding countryside, while the townspeople provided the lord of the manor with annual rents. Early and newly adapted Anglo-Norman towns were mainly located in the east, where new settlements. such as Kilkenny and Drogheda. were established. Pre-existing Danish Viking settlements, such as Dublin, Waterford, Wexford and Limerick, were also taken for the Crown.

The Normans did not take Cork so easily. The leader of the Danes, Gilbert, son of Turgarius, spearheaded a counterattack, but after a bloody battle the Danes and Native Irish were defeated. Such was the importance of this victory that a church dedicated to St Nicholas, a saint revered by the Normans, was built in 1174 off Douglas Street to commemorate the event. The present-day St Nicholas Church (1847) is the third church built on the site.

Cork became one of fifty-eight Anglo-Norman walled towns in Ireland. Initially, the Danish settlement on the marshy island was fortified and had a gate (*porta*) leading into it. The nature of the fortification, whether it was stone or timber, was not recorded. Incorporating elements of the old settlement, the newcomers made many fundamental changes to the town.

Firstly, the name of the town was shortened to Corke. The renaming was significant as it was the first instance of the anglicising of local Gaelic culture. Cork's first Royal charter was granted by Prince John in 1185. As a Royal town, Cork would enjoy similar privileges to English towns, would thrive as a centre of political and administrative control and would also receive the protection of the Crown.

In 1210 Cork County, along with eleven other counties, was made shire ground by King John, who appointed sheriffs and other proper officers to govern them. In 1241–42, Henry III granted a charter that outlined the rights of individuals living within the town, including one regulation in particular aimed to preserve the native trade. It forbade foreigners to sell cloth or wine within the town and stipulated that they could sell their wares there for not more than forty days. Furthermore, any purchase made by a foreigner had to be from a native merchant, especially if that purchase were corn, leather or wool.

The Anglo-Normans also made significant changes to the landscape of the city. Between 1170 and the 1300s, a stone wall, on average eight metres high, became the new boundary of the old Viking settlement, accessible via a new drawbridge built on the site of Droichet. Beyond this wall a suburb called Dungarvan (now the area of North Main Street) was established on a nearby island. There are few historic records describing Dungarvan. It is known that it was connected to the walled island town by a bridge and that a watermill stood between the two areas.

Three excavations in the past fifteen years have revealed evidence for the existence of Dungarvan. In 1983 a thirteenth-century mural turret was found on Corn Market Street, while in 1994 excavations on the site of Kyrl's Quay Shopping Centre uncovered a quay wall. It was at Kyrl's Quay too that excavations yielded evidence of the development of street frontages and burgage plots. These plots dated to the thirteenth century and extended from the street frontage of the houses back towards the town wall. Each of the seven plots excavated measured between six and seven metres in width, although one was eight metres wide at the street and ten metres at the rear. They were divided from each other by rubble walls. These plots were put to good use by the residents. Bake ovens, either open-air or enclosed, were a feature of some, and these possibly produced foodstuffs for commercial purposes.

With the development of the old Viking island settlement and the new satellite settlement of Dungarvan, the late thirteenth century witnessed Cork expanding rapidly as a municipal and economic centre. In 1273 the first mayor, Richard Wine, was appointed, suggesting that by that time an administrative body, such as a corporation, was in place. Economically, charter evidence describes the port at Cork as very profitable. The customs returns of Irish ports in the period 1276–1333 show that Cork was the third most important port in Ireland, after New Ross and Waterford.

A Tale of Two Islands

In 1284, King Edward I authorised the collection of additional murage tolls, or taxes, in order to extend the existing town wall to encompass Dungarvan. By 1317 the full circuit was complete. This redevelopment created a single walled settlement instead of a walled centre with an unfortified settlement and Dungarvan outside it. A

In 1996 archaeologists uncovered the foundations of Queen's Castle on Castle Street.

channel of water was left between the old walled settlement and the newly encompassed area of Dungarvan, with access between the two provided by an arched stone bridge called Middle Bridge. The town extended from South Gate Bridge to North Gate Bridge and was bisected by North and South Main Streets. These were the primary routeways and, although narrower than the current streets, would have followed an identical plan. They would also have been the main market areas. A millrace dominated the western half of this channel, while the eastern half was the location of the main dock.

The town was well defended. At regular intervals on the wall were mural towers which projected out and were used as lookout posts by the town's garrison. All those seeking to enter the town had to use one of the three designated entrances: one of the two well-fortified drawbridges, or the portcullis gate. South Gate Drawbridge gave access from the southern valleyside, while entry from the northern valleyside was via North Gate Drawbridge. Various depictions of the walled town in the late sixteenth century show the heads of executed criminals on top of the drawbridges' towers. Each head was placed on a spike, which was slotted into a rectangular slab of stone. Local tradition has it that one of the stone blocks still exists today at the top of the steps of the Counting House in Beamish and Crawford Brewery on South Main Street.

The third entrance overlooked the eastern marshes and was located at the present-day intersection of Castle Street and Grand Parade. Known as Watergate, it comprised a large portcullis gate that opened to allow ships into a small, unnamed quay located within the town. On either side of this gate two large mural towers, known as King's Castle and Queen's Castle, controlled its mechanics.

As Cork was an Anglo-Norman colonial outpost, the town was protected by a garrison of soldiers stationed near North Gate Bridge, which, like South Gate Drawbridge, was manned twenty-four hours a day. An interesting quote from an English traveller in the late fourteenth century illustrates that the inhabitants of Cork feared attacks by the Native Irish and 'were forced to watch their gates continually, to keep them shut at service times, at meals, from sunset to sun arising, nor suffer any stranger to enter them with his weapon, but to leave the same at a lodge appointed.'

In the last two decades, archaeological excavations have uncovered much important evidence within the area of the walled town. In particular, several sections of the lower courses of the town walls have been discovered along with parts of streets, laneways, houses and even the remains of past citizens. Much of the town wall survives beneath the modern street surface, and in some places has been incorporated into modern buildings.

The population of Cork c.1300 is estimated at 800 people. It is likely that wealthy Anglo-Norman families of the merchant class were the principal residents as they would have been able to afford the rents payable to the king. Some of these wealthy merchants founded the Corporation of Cork, a municipal, legal and administrative body; it is unknown when it was formed or how many members it had. Most of the corporation's public business was conducted just off South Main Street, in the area now occupied by Beamish and Crawford. The council tower, armoury, the court house, commandant's house and the treasury were all located nearby. The families involved in the government of the town included the Roches, Skiddys, Galways, Coppingers, Meades, Goulds, Tirrys, Sarsfields and Morroghs. These surnames comprised the mayoral list from the early thirteenth century until the seventeenth century.

Several archaeological excavations have revealed evidence for the construction of different types of houses within the walled town. The Anglo-Normans built post-and-wattle houses and sill-beam houses. From the fourteenth century to the sixteenth century, the majority of the houses overlooked the main streets. The building materials were all highly flammable, therefore for the first 300 years of the walled town's history it was illegal to leave a fire lighting at night – a misdemeanour punishable by a heavy fine, known as 'smoke silver'. Indeed, the building of timber houses within the walls was outlawed in May 1622 after a fire swept through the town. It was not, however, caused by mismanagement of domestic fires but by lightning. Contemporary descriptions detail that 1,500 houses were burnt down and large parts of the town were destroyed.

The *Pacata Hibernia* depiction of the walled town c.1585–1600 shows two tower houses on North Main Street. These residences, Skiddy's Castle and Roche's Castle, belonged to two wealthy and influential merchant families. In the late 1970s, excavations near North Gate Bridge revealed the base of Skiddy's Castle and a two-metre-high stone mantelpiece inscribed '1597 G.S.'. The mantelpiece was incorporated into the Centre for the Unemployed building on North Main Street, placed high above the main entrance. In 1997 the stone foundations of Roche's Castle were uncovered at the southern end of North Main Street.

Despite the wealth of the town, daily life in medieval Cork would have been harsh. Overcrowding was common in poorly ventilated dwellings, whilst the water supply was often contaminated by sewage. Household waste was thrown into the streets and dead animals were left to rot where they fell. The upper floor of the residences usually projected out into the street, blocking out the light and lending the town a gloomy aspect. The streets were poorly paved and very muddy due to tidal water seeping up through the marshy ground. The air would have been damp and heavy, and as a result many diseases were rampant, including measles, mumps, influenza, leprosy, chicken pox, scarlet fever, tuberculosis, typhus and whooping cough. All this death and misery was compounded in the mid-1300s when the Black Death crept through the town and its Liberties.

The high mortality rate was confirmed by an examination of over 200 skeletons found at Crosses Green. Three-quarters of the individuals were found to be adults, mostly aged in their twenties. Just less than half were found to have degenerative joint diseases or some

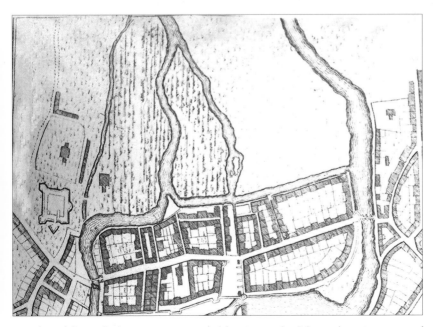

A plan of the walled town, reconstructed from an early eighteenth-century map of Cork. The north channel of the Lee is on the right-hand side.

form of arthritis, while nutritional deficiencies, tumours and dental diseases were noted in several cases.

The levels of poverty meant that crime was a serious issue. Punishments were severe, with the death penalty automatically given for serious cases. Beheading and hanging were the usual methods of execution. Up until the late 1800s, public hangings took place at Gallows Green, near the southern road leading into the town. The site is now marked by Greenmount National School and the Lough Community Centre. In 1990 a mass grave was discovered in this area containing the remains of at least fifteen individuals. All the bones were disarticulated, many were broken and in most cases they were stacked into neat piles with the skulls lying close by.

Developing a Medieval Port Town

Cork's sturdy walls and deep, sheltered harbour, combined with its rich agricultural hinterland, made the city an important strategic asset for the Crown. After the extension of the wall c.1300, several taxes are listed in subsequent Royal charters, relating to a variety of traded goods. Various cloths of English and French origin, along with foreign spices and vegetables were imported. A wide range of British ports handled these goods, including Bristol, Carlisle, Southampton and Pembroke. There are numerous references to the importation of wine from France, the main ports being Gascony, Bayonne and Bordeaux. This extensive wine trade is reflected in the vast amount of French pottery unearthed in the city. Commonly known as Saintonge pottery, the most ubiquitous type seems to have been glazed jugs of a mottled green colour.

The tax list also reveals that the principal exports were oats, wheat, beef, pork, oatmeal, fish, butter, cheese, tallow (a form of animal fat) and malt. Hides from cattle, horse, deer and goat, as well as wool were traded, along with skins from small wild animals, such as rabbit and squirrel. There is also the possibility that some live animals were exported, such as horses, cattle, sheep, pigs and goats. All trading ships had to report to the custom house that overlooked the inner dock. Here, taxes were paid on all imports and exports.

Archaeological evidence indicates the presence of several crafts within the city. The largest of these was metalworking. Large quantities of iron slag have been found, along with iron-smelting furnaces.

The most significant find was made at the Gate Cinema on Bachelor's Quay in 1994, when a blacksmith's forge was discovered dating
to the early fourteenth century.

A large amount of iron objects have also been found,
including knives, spearheads, nails, horse
tack, tools, barrel padlocks and keys.
Bronze objects such as stick-pins
(dress-fasteners), buckles, needles and
keys have been found, and lead objects,
such as lead weights. The underlying
marshy soil in the city provides perfect
conditions for the preservation of
bone artefacts and many have been
retrieved, such as bone combs
made from deer antlers, gaming
pieces, needles, spindle whorls,
harp pegs and toggles.

An everyday object from the
walled town of Cork. Ashwood
was commonly used in making
turned bowls, like this one.

Finds of wooden artefacts show that several species of native tree
were used. Each was utilised in a different way according to which
type of object was being produced. For example, oak was favoured for
the framework of buildings and for furniture. Ash was used in the
making of bowls as it was easy to carve. Yew was favoured in carving
and stave-making. Many leather artefacts, especially footwear, belts,
straps and sheaths, have also been found. The importance of the
leather industry is reflected in the fact that grants were given by
Queen Elizabeth I to the guilds of shoe-making, glove-making and
tanning in the late 1500s.

As the town developed and became *au fait* with European business
practices, a system of quality control was initiated through the establishment of guilds. Each craft within the walled town, ranging from
iron-workers to shoe-makers, had its own guild, which regulated
wages, maintained standards and supported members who fell ill.
Most guilds became quite wealthy and owned their own halls where
they held regular meetings. However, the locations of the guild
houses is not known and we do not find clues in streetnames, as is the
case in cities such as Dublin. Guilds were also widespread in English
towns and thus provided a common base for trading links.

The fourteenth century saw further advances in the development
of the walled town as an inner Atlantic port. In 1326, Cork became a

staple town, in other words, an official market for
hides, wools and woolfells (skins with wool still
attached). The regulations of a staple town were
few, but aimed to concentrate the accumulation of reve-
nue in one area and to prevent tax avoidance. For example,
citizens were only to wear cloth made in England, Ireland or
Wales, and foreign merchants could trade
in hides only in a staple town.

The spout of a tall jug. This
sherd, found at Kyrl's Quay,
is a piece of Redcliffe pottery from Bristol, produced
from the mid-thirteenth
century on.

Matters of Conquest and Colonisation, 1500–1600

At the beginning of the 1500s, the Crown
did not have much power in Ireland. Rebellions during the previous centuries had
been so successful that by the time Henry VIII took the throne in
1509, the Native Irish chieftains held almost all of Ulster, Connacht,
north and west Munster, the midlands and part of the east coast
between Dublin and Wexford.

The accession of King Henry VIII to the throne was to change many
aspects of Anglo-Irish relations. A Royal survey in 1515 revealed that
in several counties bribes were being paid to Irish chieftains to buy
their goodwill. For example, the citizens of Cork were paying the
McCarthy chieftain forty pounds a year for immunity from attack. It
was also revealed that many English settlers had integrated alarm-
ingly well into Irish culture. In some instances, they were going so far
as to make peace with the Irish without the prior consent of the king.
This survey called for radical political change.

The subsequent reforms included the forcible introduction of a
new religion – the Church of England. The first effects of the Reformation were felt in Cork in the 1540s when the abbeys of the Franciscans, Augustinians and Dominicans were forced to close. The
monasteries' possessions were confiscated and redistributed among
the wealthy supporters of the Crown. In response, there were local-
ised rebellions all over the country.

During Edward's reign, English power declined further, but the
reign of Queen Mary brought hope for the Catholic population. This
hope faded rapidly after 1558 when she died and Elizabeth, her Protestant step-sister, became queen. Elizabeth I re-enacted the Act of

Supremacy – a strong policy of colonial control – and passed several other regulations to increase the monarchy's jurisdiction in Ireland. However, her laws succeeded only in those areas where English dominance was strongest, such as Dublin and The Pale, while elsewhere the Irish chieftains continued to hold sway.

To counteract this, Elizabeth initiated the Plantation, sending English farmers to live and work on Irish land. In places such as Cork, pardons and financial compromises were offered to powerful clans, such as the O'Sullivans and the McCarthys, to persuade them to accept this new regime. The Catholic clergy, however, was immune to such promises and priests continued to say Mass openly.

The discovery of the Americas quickened the Empire's desire for power, especially through trading links, and England vied with Spain for control of the maritime trading routes. The tension between the two escalated in July 1588 when the Spanish Armada, the largest naval force ever seen, sailed into view of England's coast. Elizabeth sent Sir Francis Drake to repel the attack. Using clever tactical manoeuvres, the English gained the upper hand. During the battle, however, five of Drake's ships of war were pursued into Cork Harbour by the Spanish. The English sailed up the Carrigaline River and anchored under Currabinny Hill. The Spaniards entered the river in pursuit, but failed to find them and sailed out again. The placename Drake's Pool marks Drake's safe hiding place.

To protect Cork from further Spanish incursions, two fortifications were constructed: Blackrock Castle and Elizabeth Fort. Blackrock Castle was built in 1582 and has been reconstructed twice, in 1722 and 1827. In recent times it has been purchased by Cork City Council (formerly Cork Corporation) and is awaiting redevelopment. Elizabeth Fort, an earthen embanked fort named in honour of the queen, was constructed in 1601.

As well as the new fortifications there was Shandon Castle, overlooking the main approach road known as Mallow Lane, now Shandon Street. In 1177 the castle had been the stronghold of Diarmuid McCarthy, but was taken over by the Anglo-Normans. It passed through a number of hands, but in the early 1500s was owned by the Barry family. A *Pacata Hibernia* map depicts the castle as having two large towers adjoined to each other, one larger than the other.

Despite the feuds and political machinations, sixteenth-century Cork was also a place of genteel pursuits. For the wealthy, there were

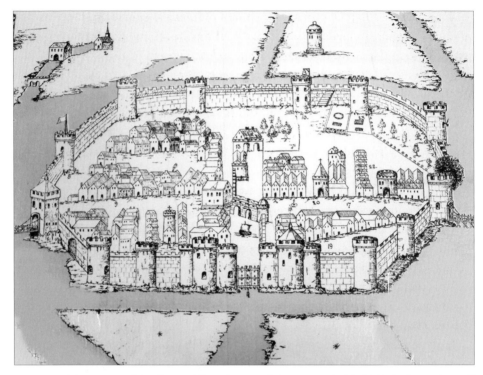

A later copy of the *Pacata Hibernia* map of the town *c*.1585–1600. It shows the wall encompassing two island settlements – the original town and Dungarvan – with associated entrances. The walled defences provided security for the inhabitants until 1690.

many pleasurable diversions, such as reading and hunting. The city enjoyed the presence of famous personages, most notably the eminent poet Edmund Spencer, who spent nineteen years in Cork. His residence was the Castle of Kilcolman near Doneraile in north Cork. In 1580, Spencer was appointed secretary to Lord Grey, the Lord Deputy of Ireland. In the 1590s Spencer married Elizabeth Boyle in the medieval Church of St FinBarre. It was also in Cork that he wrote his famous poem, 'The Faerie Queen'.

Seventeenth-century Cork: Towards a Resolution

The problems arising from English colonisation continued into the early 1600s. Many Irish Catholics felt strong resentment towards the Crown. They refused to accept the new Protestant religion and as a result small, violent rebellions were common. It was at this time that Cork became known as the 'Rebel County'. By the late 1600s, two

Irish chieftains, Hugh O'Neill and Red Hugh O'Donnell, were waging all-out war against Queen Elizabeth. O'Neill was in communication with Spain and received occasional aid in the form of arms and monies. Requests for a Spanish force to be sent to Ireland were finally honoured by Philip III, and on 23 September 1601 a Spanish fleet arrived at Kinsale Harbour and took the town and its environs. The English responded by sending 2,000 men to join the 7,000 already stationed in Cork, and the town became a crucial pawn in the attack on the Spanish invaders.

Arriving at Kinsale, O'Neill's army attempted to join the Spanish contingent, but were outmanoeuvred by English despatches and forced to retreat. The English prepared for a lengthy siege of the Spaniards' positions at Kinsale, Baltimore, Castlehaven and Berehaven. In January 1602, Don Juan Del Áquila agreed to evacuate his troops and the joint Spanish–Irish campaign came to an end. In April 1603, Queen Elizabeth I died and a new Protestant king, James I, was proclaimed.

In the first decade of the seventeenth century the town boundaries were changed. A charter granted by King James I in 1608 officially extended the limits of municipal jurisdiction by a radius of approximately three miles beyond the settlement. This area became known as the 'County of the City of Cork'. The subsequent increase in trade meant that a large new dock was needed. It was constructed on the edges of one of the marshes to the east of the town.

Building works to accommodate the increased level of trade were necessary throughout the seventeenth century. On 14 November 1639, for instance, Cork Corporation agreed to build North Gate Bridge with 'good and sound timber' and to pave it with sand. They also decided to put similar paving on South Gate Bridge. New drawbridge towers were also to be built on the bridges, and the river channels were to be cleaned of rubbish.

King James I was replaced by his son, Charles I, in 1624. Fearing another Spanish–Irish attack, Charles attempted to win the support of Irish Catholic

The first Royal mint was established in Cork in 1295. The coins it produced were inscribed, *Civitas Corciae*. The silver coins shown above, found in this Bellarmine jar during an excavation on Grattan Street, span a period of 220 years.

landlords. He rejected the Oath of Supremacy, to which Roman Catholics objected on religious grounds, in favour of an Oath of Allegiance. Influential Protestant families, such as the Inchiquins and Broghills, publicly questioned Charles's strategy. They launched a letter campaign to persuade the monarch to change his approach, but their pleas were ignored. Over time, this situation had a detrimental effect on the financial and social position of the Protestant settlers in Cork.

By January 1649 the King's own parliament had turned against him and the MPs ordered his capture and execution. Britain thus became a republic. The Parliamentarians sent a force to Ireland to suppress any pro-Royal sympathy. The army was led by the new Lord Lieutenant of Ireland, Oliver Cromwell.

Cromwell arrived in Ireland on 15 August 1649 and took control of the town of Drogheda after a bloody massacre. He then proceeded to Wexford and New Ross and sent out small contingents into the Munster countryside to take note of any pro-Royalist military activity. In October 1649 Cork Corporation surrendered before Cromwell even arrived in the area, such was the fear of slaughter. From 1649 to 1683, the Catholic citizens of Cork lived under severe restrictions and were monitored in all aspects of their daily lives.

In 1683 a new Catholic king ascended the throne, King James II. The English parliament objected to the new monarch and offered the throne to the Dutch prince, William of Orange. James was forced to flee to Ireland and in March 1688 he arrived at Cork and incited the people to rise up against the Protestant pretender. In the spring of 1689, William led a huge army to Ireland to restore power.

The first confrontation between the Jacobites and Williamites occurred in 1690 on the banks of the River Boyne in County Meath, where the Jacobites were defeated. James fled south and sailed into exile. After the Battle of the Boyne, William turned his attention to the walled town of Limerick, which was also occupied by supporters of James II. However, he failed to take the town and was forced to retreat. At the same time, rebellions against the Williamites escalated in south Munster. The English forces were far better equipped and more numerous and therefore were easily able to quash any insurrection.

In September 1690 a Jacobite army along with a number of Irish rebel factions joined forces to take control of Cork to provide a stronghold position against King William. The actual number of

insurgents is not recorded, but it is likely that several hundred soldiers were involved in the takeover of the walled town. These forces
were welcomed by the Catholics in the area. They manned the drawbridges and the town wall-walks, readied numerous buildings and
waited for the attack they knew must surely come.

The defence of the town was important throughout its history, particularly in the seventeenth
century. Built in 1601, Elizabeth Fort – its massive walls visible above the town in the photograph shown – was a vital strategic stronghold.

The Siege of Cork 1690

In September 1690, King William despatched a large contingent of
men to regain control of Cork. They arrived in Cork Harbour with
over eighty ships and approximately 5,000 men. A landing was
opposed at Passage by Irish rebels who possessed a battery of seven or
eight cannons. However, they were soon overrun by several armed
boats sent ashore to deal with this opposition.

The next day a regiment of about 800 men marched through
Douglas and camped in the area of the Lough. Again the rebels
attempted to block their passage but were shot down. Meanwhile,
the English planned to exploit the main defensive disadvantage of the
walled area: its low-lying position overlooked by hills. Control of the
hills would mean control of the walled town.

After advancing on the southern environs of the town, the English regiment set their sights on Cat Barracks, which was adjacent to the southern road leading to South Gate Drawbridge. This small barracks, constructed in 1685 by Thomas Philips, was used as a storage depot for the firearms of nearby Elizabeth Fort. The rebels retreated into the town as the English advanced, setting fire to the southern suburbs as they did so, around the area now occupied by Douglas Street, Cove Street and Barrack Street.

In the afternoon of 23 September 1690 the English cannons were transferred to Fair Hill, just to the west of present-day Commons Road, in an attempt to mount an assault on Shandon Castle. The rebels again set fire to the suburbs, this time around Shandon, and retreated within the safety of the town walls.

On 25 September, 200 foot soldiers advanced on Cat Barracks and, finding it deserted, immediately took possession of it. At this time the focus of the attack moved to Elizabeth Fort, the stronghold of the Jacobite side. During the night, the attackers moved closer to the fort and hid themselves in ditches and laneways.

On 26 September constant bombardment of Elizabeth Fort resulted in the collapse of the wall above its gate and part of the adjacent bastion. Shells from a mortar were fired into the city, killing two or three people. Meanwhile, on the northside, an advance was made on Shandon Castle, which was also found to be deserted.

On 27 September the bombardment of the city escalated. The cannons concentrated on breaching the eastern wall, a point now marked by the City Library on the Grand Parade. It was decided that the spire of St FinBarre's Cathedral be used as a vantage point from which to fire into the town, and a musket gun was quickly mounted on top of the spire. The first casualty of the 'sniper' fire was the governor of Elizabeth Fort. In retaliation, the Jacobite soldiers aimed two guns at the steeple and shook it immensely.

After a few more days of sustained attack, the rebels within the walled town surrendered. The key figures on the rebel side were summarily executed, along with several members of their families, and the suburbs were burned and destroyed. Elizabeth Fort was surrendered within one hour of the signing of the agreement, as stipulated, and the town gates were surrendered the following Monday morning at eight o'clock. All arms and ammunition were left in a secure place for the English to collect. The siege would prove to be a major catalyst in initiating change in the physical and social landscape of the city.

Two interesting remnants of the siege can be seen in the city. On the corner of Grand Parade and Tuckey Street is a cannon reputedly used in the battle; it is thought that it was later used as a mooring post for a quayside in the 1700s. The second is a cannon ball fired from Elizabeth Fort at the tower of St FinBarre's Cathedral. During the rebuilding of the cathedral in 1735–38, this twenty-four-pound cannon ball was found embedded in the spire. It is now on display in the ambulatory of the cathedral.

A remnant from the Siege of Cork 1690, this cannon is now on display at the corner of Tuckey Street and Grand Parade.

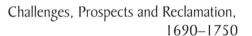

Challenges, Prospects and Reclamation, 1690–1750

The signing of the Treaty of Limerick in October 1691 marked the final victory of the Williamite side over the Jacobites. The Jacobite soldiers were expelled from Ireland in an event known as the Flight of the Wild Geese. One-seventh of the land was left in Catholic hands, the rest was confiscated and given to loyal Protestants. To safeguard its control in Ireland, the Crown introduced the Penal Laws. These laws were a form of sectarian cleansing, designed to eliminate Catholicism as a political force. The measures included depriving Catholics access to educational facilities and public professions. Although designed to suppress Catholic worship too, small Masshouses did hold services in the city.

It was in the eighteenth century too that Cork began to be generally referred to as a city. After 1690, the roll call of mayors and sheriffs suggests a new ruling class. The names of old English merchant families, such as the Galways, Skiddys, Roches, Goulds, Meades, Coppingers and Tirrys, disappear and the new surnames of mercantile families are recorded, including Maylor, Winthrop, Tuckey, Lavitt, Pembroke, Brocklesby and Deane.

In the winter of 1690, the Penal Laws were just one concern of the Corporation and the citizens. The siege had left the town in ruins and it fell to the Corporation to rebuild it. Four main issues needed to be addressed: the breaches in the wall; the increasing number of requests to build houses against the inner face of the wall; the construction of new quays; and the rebuilding of the central core of the town. The decisions made in the 1690s by Cork Corporation resulted in changes that fashioned the city centre as we know it today.

For nearly 500 years, the town wall had symbolised the urbanity of

Once the centre of eighteenth-century expansion, the narrow lane of French Church Street is an interesting mix of old and modern.

Cork and had given its citizens a distinct identity. But that was set to change as the process of modernisation began. In the first decade of the 1700s large portions of the town wall were dismantled, especially the eastern portion, the lower courses of which are now preserved in Bishop Lucey Park. Quays and bridges were built on the western edges of the town, connecting the marshes to the west and east. At this time a second group emerged to work alongside the Corporation for the good of the city. Members of the Huguenot and the Quaker communities set about reclaiming large areas of marshland to the west and east of the town and started to build on those areas.

By the mid-1700s, over 300 Huguenots had established themselves in the city, primarily involved in textile manufacture. Huguenot families such as the Lavitts, who built Lavitt's Quay in 1704, made important contributions to the layout of the town. The areas of French Church Street, Carey's Lane and Academy Street in the city centre are located where the core of the Huguenot quarter would have been.

To the west of the crumbling walled town, the Quakers also reclaimed and developed large areas of marshy lands. This community had been in Cork since 1655, but it was only in the early 1700s that they were granted the right to develop their own lands. One of the first Quaker pioneers in the development of the western marshes was Joseph Pike, who purchased marshland in 1696, now the area of Grattan Street. Another key player was John Haman, a respected linen merchant. Minor players included the Devonshire family, the Sleigh family and the Fenn family (Fenn's Quay marks their land).

In general, four main developments occurred on the bought, or leased-out marshes. The first was the building of residences there. Buildings constructed overlooking the quays had steps leading up to their front doors in order to prevent flooding from channel water. This feature can still be seen on the South Mall and on St Patrick's Street today.

The second development was the construction of streets or roads adjacent to these houses. These were wide thoroughfares with minor streets running off them at right angles. Thirdly, quays were constructed at the edge of the developed marshes, giving access to the islands themselves. On what is now the South Mall, a quay known as The Mall became the principal promenade of the gentry classes. Fourthly, several unnamed arched stone bridges were also built connecting the marshes to each other and to the adjacent hillsides. The drawbridges of South Gate Bridge and North Gate Bridge were taken down around 1712 and replaced by arched stone bridges.

The year 1714 saw the accession of George I to the throne and a period of prosperity for the Protestant Ascendancy. High-profile Protestants held a monopoly in Irish politics, society and economy. The upper merchant classes adopted a grand style in all aspects of their lives. The Royal Cork Yacht Club, founded in 1720 and the oldest yacht club in Britain and Ireland, typified the leisurely life of the rich.

In 1715 work began on a new North Gate Jail, as well as on the Green-Coat Hospital and School in Shandon. The school was initiated by Rev. Dr Henry Maule. St Anne's Church, Shandon, was constructed in 1722 under the direction of the Protestant Bishop, Peter Browne. Adjacent to St Anne's was Skiddy's Almshouse, founded in 1717 at the behest of the Skiddy family. Now a residential home for the elderly, it was built with an arcade of semicircular

South Gate Bridge (*above*) replaced the old South Gate Drawbridge that allowed access into the walled town from the southern approach road.

arches. A corn market was constructed in 1719 overlooking a square that was located on a filled-in section of the River Lee. Unfortunately, the name of this square is not recorded, but it was located on what is now Corn Market Street. Over the centuries, the square became the traditional central market area of the city. It would have been thronged with dealers and customers, selling and buying anything from a needle to an anchor. Several stalls still operate there today.

A report by two unnamed touring Englishmen in 1748 noted that the economy of Cork was booming and that provisions of all kinds were available at reasonable prices, including meat, fish, fowl, fruits, such as strawberries, and tubers. Their closing remarks on Cork are very interesting – they noted that Cork people had no recognisable accent, which points to a great mix of nationalities residing and trading in the city.

In 1719 a large section of marshy land, now the area of Fitzgerald's Park, was bought by the town clerk, Edward Webber, a Dutchman. He decided to build a raised walkway across this land at his own expense. He called it the Meer-Dyke, which translates roughly as 'an embankment to protect the land from the sea'. While constructing the walk, Webber also built a red-brick tea house, the first of its kind in Cork.

Fruit gardens, pathways of gravel and stone seats were put down. The tea house soon became a fashionable meeting place for the wealthy. After Webber's death in 1735, his tea house and gardens continued to prosper until the mid-1740s when they were closed down. James Morrison, mayor of Cork in 1784, bought the tea house and gardens and had the grounds professionally landscaped. The house is now occupied by the Sacred Heart College.

In 1720 the town's custom house was relocated from lower St Patrick's Street to what is now the premises of the Crawford Municipal Art Gallery on Emmet Place. Part of the 1720 structure is still visible on Emmet Place, adjacent to Cork Opera House.

Under the supervision of Bishop Browne, several churches were reconstructed in the 1720s. These included St Peter's Church, Christ Church, the Church of St Nicholas and St FinBarre's Cathedral. A new church, St Paul's, was constructed in 1723 to provide ecclesiastical services to the many sailors passing through Cork. St Paul's Church still exists today, adjacent to Paul Street Shopping Centre. In the grounds of the church there is a large number of sailors' graves because one mayor of the city, Edward Brocklesby, granted free burials here to foreign sailors.

The style of the church is simple, borrowing largely from the Grecian style. It has a pitched roof and is rectangular in plan. The interior is quite beautiful. The stuccowork on the ceiling is reputed to be the work of Italian prisoners of war who were captured during the Napoleonic Wars. There is an accomplished stained-glass window depicting the Last Supper. In the vestry are the old wooden stocks, once used to hold criminals while a crowd pelted them with rotten food. St Paul's Church is now under the protection of Cork Civic Trust, and is closed to the public for the foreseeable future.

Mid-Eighteenth-century Society

By the mid-eighteenth century, Cork was a prosperous, wealthy city. Although the merchant classes were enjoying this time of plenty, life for the lower classes was not as easy. In 1730 the population was 56,000, by 1790 it had increased to 73,000. This was a significant increase in a relatively short period of time; 100 years earlier, in 1690, the population had been just 20,000.

This population explosion caused many social problems. In the early 1740s Mayor Hugh Winter was forced to employ fifteen watchmen to patrol the city between eleven o'clock and sunrise to protect the citizens. Eleven o'clock was the city's curfew, and any person caught outdoors after that time faced prosecution, or expulsion. Robbery was common, with money and clothing often reported missing. Items such as silk, lead and swords were targetted by thieves too, and the raiding of cellars for food was common.

Another problem was the number of destitute children left homeless on the streets. On the western side of the south suburbs there was a long row of cabins called the Devil's Drop. Here, the doors were thronged with half-starved children. On 12 March 1747 a workhouse was opened on what is now Leitrim Street. Local churchwardens handed over all abandoned children (foundlings) into the care of the Board of Governors, who ensured they were clothed, nursed, taught to read and write and educated in the Protestant religion. Other charitable foundations were also working to relieve poverty in the city. The Blue Coat Hospital cared for homeless children, and the Green Coat Hospital provided schooling. Bertridge's Almshouse, Captain Thomas Deane's foundation and Archdeacon Pomroy's school just east of St FinBarre's Church all attempted to help those in need.

A report published in 1750 by Dr Charles Smith gave a detailed account of the history of Cork City and County. Smith detailed the expansion of the city in the preceding decades. In particular, he highlighted the building of the many quays, the most notable being Custom House Quay (now Emmet Place), the Coal Quay, or Ferry Quay, Kyrl's Quay and North Quay (now Pope's Quay). The largest canal in the city was that which is now covered by St Patrick's Street – picture the footpaths on this street as the location of the old quaysides and the road as the canal.

As for contemporary Cork, Smith concerned himself first with the unhealthy and unsightly state of the city. He mentioned a report by a Dr Rogers, which outlined that great quantities of filth and animal entrails were spread over the streets, leading to outbreaks of diseases such as smallpox. This description was backed by a another report in 1750, given by a touring English gentleman, who described the streets of Cork as being narrow, dirty and badly lit.

In stark contrast to these scenes of degradation were Smith's descriptions of the areas frequented by the wealthy. He tells of a large

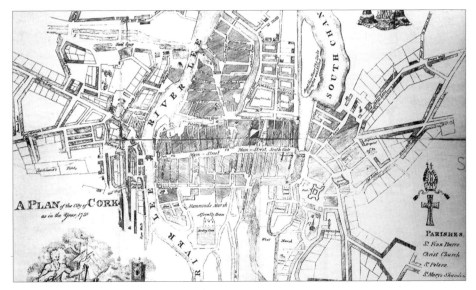

Charles Smith's map of Cork, 1750. Note the expansion to the west and east of the former walled town and the many canals, quays and residences.

bowling green with trees planted along its margin, which was located in the newly developed western marshes. The trees created a shaded promenade and bands played music to entertain the walkers. A weekly concert was held; the entry fees collected were donated to the infirmary. There were also two theatres. One was located on Duncombe's Marsh, around present-day Princes Street, and it hosted the King's Company from Dublin who performed annually in midsummer. The second was located in Broad Lane and was home to the Cork Company of players. There was also a weekly assembly and Academy of Music.

Smith also described the daily lives of the privileged. They lived in the mansions on the outskirts of the town, were attended by servants and carried out their leisure activities in their elaborate gardens and plantations. Indeed, Smith compared the banks of the River Lee to the River Seine in Paris and the River Thames in London, albeit on a smaller scale. On the northside of the city, Smith noted there was a nice hamlet with several houses and pleasant gardens known as Sunday's Well. He also mentioned large plantations of chilli and hautboy strawberries, now reflected in the placename, Strawberry Hill.

In the late 1750s one of Cork's most famous daughters, Nano Nagle, began her work with the poor. After years spent at a convent in

Paris, Nano returned to Cork in 1754 to fulfil her vocation to provide
education and instruction in the Catholic faith. Her first school was a
little rented cabin on Cobh Street, now Douglas Street. She provided
food and medicine as well as classes in reading and writing. Over time
she won the respect and support of many, eventually establishing her
own convent in 1776 called the Sisters of the Charitable Instruction
of the Sacred Heart of Jesus, better known as the Presentation
Sisters. Nano Nagle died on 26 April 1784 aged sixty-five years, and
her final resting place can be seen in the grounds of the Presentation
Convent, which is still in use. An associated primary school, run by
the Presentation order, is Cork's oldest operational school. On the
south channel of the River Lee is the Nano Nagle Footbridge, which
opened in 1985.

Forming the Modern Streetscape

In October 1760 a statue of King George astride his horse was placed
in the city to symbolise England's authority. The statue, which was
yellow and hollow, was erected in the centre of Tuckey's Bridge, now
the site of the Berwick Fountain. Vandalised in 1867 by anti-
Royalists, the only remnants of this statue can be seen in the Cork
Public Museum. It is also remembered in the Irish name of the Grand
Parade, *Sráid An Chapaill Buí*, or Street of the Yellow Horse.

In the late 1700s Cork was well represented in a number of paintings and maps. The most detailed of the paintings was John Butt's
Cork (c.1750), which is on display in the Crawford Municipal Art
Gallery. Butt depicted a myriad of quays and canals in the city, particularly highlighting the former quays and canal which were present
on what is now St Patrick's Street. On either side of the canal, merchants built two-storey warehouses. Goods were held on the ground
floor, while staff occupied the first floor. The warehouses had outside
staircases giving access to the first floor, an example of which can
still be seen at the charming Château Bar. The leases of many of the
houses along St Patrick's Street still contain clauses protecting the
lessee's right to the use of the quay outside, while others retain the
right to use stairways to reach their boats.

As the eighteenth century progressed, it became clear that the
medieval fabric of the city could not cope with the demands of the
population, and the Corporation came under pressure to improve the

situation. Fines were placed on illegal dumping, and scavengers, wheelbarrow men and street-sweepers were employed to keep the streets clean. In 1765 a commission was established to deal with the problems facing the expanding city, especially in relation to the health risks posed by inadequate facilities. Known as the Wide Streets Commission, it was first set up in Dublin. In Cork, its primary task was to widen the medieval laneways and to lay out new, wider streets for the benefit of the citizens.

Sixteen commissioners were appointed in 1765, but due to financial restrictions it was the early nineteenth century before they made an impact. At that time streets such as South

Fenn's Quay shows the style of house being built by the middle classes in eighteenth-century Cork.

Terrace and Dunbar Street were laid out, while streets such as Shandon Street were widened. In 1780 the Corporation decided to fill in the city's canals by building large culverts, or covered underground channels. Wide thoroughfares, based on the European model, were subsequently created, such as St Patrick's Street, Grand Parade and the South Mall.

There was also an increase in the number of residences built in the suburbs, a clustering recorded on road maps drawn up by cartographers Taylor and Skinner in 1777. To the northwest of the city a large estate called Fair Hill was marked as the property of the Longfield family. To the northeast, six large houses were shown adjacent to the road to Youghal, all overlooking the River Lee where it entered Cork

Harbour. The respective families who lived here were the Lombards, Newenhams, Pembrokes, Corkers, St Ledgers and Rogers. The construction of St Patrick's Bridge on the North Channel encouraged development to the northeast of the city centre, and new residences appeared on St Patrick's Hill, Camden Quay and Sidney Place. Clarke's Bridge, constructed in 1776, spanned the south channel. The structure of this bridge has remained unaltered since its initial construction.

In the Blackrock area numerous estates appeared on the landscape. The most impressive mansions included *Bessbora,* owned by the Allen family, and *Hettyfield,* owned by the Tavis family. Both Hettyfield and Bessbora are retained in placenames in the area. Douglas on the south side also boasted large estates, including *Donnybrook, Mountpellier, Barnhill, Newberry* and *Mounthovel.* Southwest of the city the large mansion and demesne *Ballinaspaig* was the property of the Protestant Bishop of Cork, Isaac Mann. Other large houses in this area include *Chetwynd, Graandarough, Doughcloyne, Wiltown, Summerstown* and *Glasheen,* their names echoing the influences of other cultures, such as Welsh.

In the late 1700s the city was booming economically. Cork's export trade comprised 40% of the national total. Just over 70% of all goods exported went to the European mainland, while Cork held 80% of the total Irish export to England's colonies, trading with ports such as Carolina, New York and the West Indies. By 1800, Cork was reputed to be the busiest transatlantic port in operation.

In 1788 a new indoor market was established in the city, which sold fresh fruit, meat and vegetables. Still located on the Grand Parade and specialising in the same produce as in 1788, the English Market is one of the city's most vibrant and popular institutions. The origin of the name 'English Market' is unknown, but it is here that you can find a Cork delicacy for the more adventurous diner – tripe and *drisheen,* or tripe and lamb's liver.

Architects of a New Age

The advent of the nineteenth century brought a change in political circumstances for Ireland and for Cork. The fear of further rebellions against British rule led to the Act of Union in 1800. This was a seismic event in Irish history. The act abolished the separate Irish

Nathaniel Grogan's painting shows North Gate Bridge in the late eighteenth century. The arched entrance on the far side leads into North Gate Jail, which served as the city jail at that time.

Parliament in Dublin, and from then until 1922 Ireland was governed directly from Westminster. Cork Corporation and the mercantile class supported the Union because it led to increased trade with Britain. This unpopular stance made the city vulnerable to attack, so a new barracks, Victoria Barracks, was constructed in 1806. It is now called Collins Barracks (after Michael Collins).

Britain also benefitted from the Act of Union. The early nineteenth century was a turbulent time in northwest Europe, with conflict between Britain and France. This resulted in reduced imports from the European mainland to Britain, leaving Britain with an urgent need to find new trading partners. Cork was to fulfil this need. Cork possessed the largest shambles, or slaughtering houses, in Ireland. The slaughtering season started in September and continued to the end of January. One observer recorded that 100,000 black cattle were killed and cured each year, largely for export to Britain.

The end of the Napoleonic Wars in 1815 exposed many of the hidden dilemmas within Cork's economy. A general recession ensued and there was little demand for Irish products. Where a demand did exist, export profits were low as prices fell. For example, between 1818 and 1822 grain prices were halved, while the price of beef and pork fell by about one-third.

For the working classes, the post-war period brought large-scale unemployment, especially for those previously involved in the provision trade. The resultant fall in income meant food was scarce and housing conditions deteriorated. This in turn led to epidemics such as typhoid sweeping through the city. In the *Statistical Survey of County Cork* (1815), Horatio Townsend highlighted the huge gap that existed between the middle and lower classes. He placed particular emphasis on the need for moving people out of the slum areas of North and South Main Streets, and Barrack Street on the southside and Shandon Street on the northside. The housing crisis was exacerbated by the influx of rural labourers into the city, who arrived in search of work and food. As a result, there were an extra 10,000 people residing in the city in 1821, bringing the population to approximately 100,000 without any concomitant increase in the housing capacity.

In 1822 the British economy began to recover and funds were made available for Irish issues. The Wide Streets Commission was reinstigated after an absence of nearly half a century. One of the main projects undertaken was the destruction of the large slum areas around South Main Street. Consequently, the boulevard-style Great George's Street was opened in November 1824. (It was renamed Washington Street after 1922.)

Work on a new road, known as the Western Road, commenced in 1821 and was completed by 1831. It joined Great George's Street to a new bridge named Brunswick Bridge (now O'Neil Crowley Bridge), which spanned the south channel of the River Lee. The bridge, designed by the Pain brothers, has three segmental arches. Other municipal initiatives involved the introduction of gas lighting into the city in June 1825 and the extension of the Western Road across part of the Mardyke to the north channel of the River Lee. Another arched stone bridge was built in 1826. It was known as Wellington Bridge, later renamed Thomas Davis Bridge.

The availability of funding allowed another institution, the Cork Harbour Commissioners, established in 1813, to carry out essential work on the quaysides and harbour. A large majority of the parapet walls that guarded the quays were replaced by limestone pillars. In addition, a new custom house was constructed in 1814 adjacent to

Anderson's Quay. That building is still used by the Port of Cork Company, the new name of the Harbour Commissioners.

From the 1830s onwards, elaborate municipal buildings and elegant streetscapes were constructed. Banks, a City Courthouse, a new City Jail and a new County Jail were all built at this time, along with many Catholic churches thanks to the Catholic Emancipation Act 1829. The design of many of the public buildings was the work of two families: the Pains and the Deanes. Rivalling each other in talent and ambition, they accepted contracts on behalf of public bodies and from private individuals.

James and George Richard Pain were responsible for many of the finest buildings in the city. They redesigned SS Mary and Anne's North Cathedral and Blackrock Castle after they were gutted by fire in 1827. During the 1830s they designed Holy Trinity Church (Catholic), St Patrick's Church (Catholic) and St Luke's Church (Anglican) as well as the new City Courthouse. George Richard Pain was elected Freeman of the city of Cork in 1827.

Thomas Deane was the Pains's equal in terms of contribution to the city's architectural heritage. He designed the Commercial Buildings on the South Mall, later the Imperial Hotel, and the City Jail at Shanakiel. In 1823 he also designed his own large mansion, located adjacent to an old fifteenth-century tower house at Dundanion, Blackrock, in the southern suburbs. His house was burnt down in 1900 and immediately rebuilt, and is still occupied today. He also designed St Mary's Dominican Church on Pope's Quay, the Trustee Savings Bank on Lapp's Quay and the Quadrangle at UCC.

Blackrock Castle: originally a basic stone watchtower constructed in 1585, it was remodelled by George Richard Pain in 1829 after it burnt down.

Fr Theobald Mathew: 'Apostle of Temperance'

Early merchandising in nineteenth-century Cork, promoting Fr Mathew's temperance campaign.

In the 1830s and 1840s one of Cork's most famous characters came to prominence, Fr Theobald Mathew. His best-known contribution to society was the creation of an effective temperance movement. Among the many social problems afflicting the country in the first half of the 1800s, drunkenness was a serious issue. Cheap to purchase, whiskey was the common choice across the classes. The idea of teetotalism filtered in from England, where many impoverished people had turned to alcohol to escape their problems, leading to an increase in alcohol-related illnesses and social disorder. The temperance movement aimed to tackle and eradicate this pattern by urging members to 'take the pledge', that is, to swear to abstain from alcohol.

Fr Mathew made it his life's mission to make this movement a success in Ireland. By 1839 teetotalism had gained widespread popular support. Indeed, by the end of 1840, 180,000–200,000 people nationwide had taken the pledge and Fr Mathew was acclaimed as the 'Apostle of Temperance'. In the late 1840s Fr Mathew went to America to rally support for his temperance movement there, and in his absence the cause in Ireland and England suffered. By 1850, teetotalism had lost its hold on the population.

Fr Mathew died at Queenstown, now Cobh, in December 1856. His remains were buried in his own cemetery in Cork, St Joseph's Cemetery, which he had created for the poor. He is remembered in Cork through events like *Féis Matiú*, which takes place in Fr Mathew Hall on Fr Mathew Street. William O'Connor, a merchant tailor in the city and a contemporary admirer of Fr. Mathew, erected the Fr. Mathew Tower at Dunsland, Glanmire, in 1843. But by far the most well-known commemorative feature in the city is the statue of Fr Mathew erected in 1864 on St Patrick's Street.

Pre-Famine Cork – the Seeds of a Crisis

By 1840 the population of the city had dropped to 80,000, a decrease of 20,000 in just twenty years. This fall-off was probably due to emigration as the citizens opted to take their chances elsewhere and leave their declining city. One can appreciate their despair: the classes were still divided by huge differences in wealth, the city was still overcrowded, the economy had been unstable since the Act of Union, and the poor were still hungry and forgotten.

In 1840 there was only one institution dedicated to helping the impoverished – the House of Industry, located in Blackpool and built in 1777. It was usually packed to capacity, with inmates often obliged to sleep in the open air. Large numbers were turned away each day.

Many citizens appealed to Cork Corporation to improve the conditions in which they were living; houses were ruinous with no proper facilities, such as running water or toilets. On 31 July 1838, Westminster Parliament passed the Irish Poor Relief Act and the House of Industry was chosen as the site of the new Cork Union Workhouse.

Attempts to improve the city and life for its inhabitants were hindered by political rivalry and religious division. Membership of Cork Corporation was restricted to merchants, manufacturers and professionals who were primarily Protestant. However, the Municipal Reform Act 1840 gave Protestants and Catholics equal access to local politics. In truth, however, there was bitter division on the question of municipal power. Many Protestants supported the Act of Union, while their Catholic counterparts wished to see it repealed. This meant that commercial and political relations between the two groups were strained, and they did not socialise together. The solving of local, communal problems suffered as a result.

The situation in the city was getting steadily worse. By 1840 there were 1,750 inmates in the workhouse. Many citizens were facing starvation as unemployment soared. No one then could have foreseen that what was a crisis was about to become a catastrophe.

Advent of the Famine Years

Reports of potato blight were first heard in autumn 1845. The potato had long been the staple food of the Irish people, both rich and poor,

The remains of the famine-stricken city: the ghostly archway of All Saints Cemetery on Carr's Hill. It is not known how many people are buried in this Famine graveyard.

and without it, the country was facing a famine unlike any ever endured previously.

Local relief committees, uniting all classes and creeds, were set up. The Cork Relief Committee was officially established in April 1846 and bought sacks of Indian meal from the English government and sold them at a reduced price to the citizens. The Committee set up various relief schemes in the city, such as building a wide path around the Lough, constructing a new road from the Lough to Pouladuff Road, plus stone-breaking and white-washing schemes. Despite their best efforts, they could not keep up with the demand for food.

In 1846 the entire harvest failed again. Reports of deprivation in country areas became worse each day and people from rural areas continued to pour into the city to inhabit the laneways and alleys.

The Cork Relief Committee responded by stepping up its efforts. It requested that extra food be distributed and that financial help be given to local committees to purchase and store supplies. However, price of Indian meal increased considerably and merchants began to price-fix, making it extremely difficult for the Committee to satisfy the demand. It called for government grants for public works, to provide jobs; it had 700 men on its books seeking work. Several new projects were approved, the most important being the improvement of the city's sewerage system and streets, and the provision of wash-houses for the poor.

The Cork Harbour Board contributed by employing 100 men to work on building roads, for example, the Carrigrohane Straight Road. There was also work in stone-breaking for a new public park, now Páirc Uí Chaoimh. The repair of the Navigation Wall (now the Marina) and quay works on the northside of the river employed a further 1,000 people. Other relief works included building the military prison in the Cork Barracks (now Collins Barracks), the Cork Lunatic Asylum (now in UCC) and Queen's College (now UCC). New city markets were also built and work commenced on a new railway.

In November 1846 city officials recorded 5,000 people begging on the streets. As winter set in, soup kitchens were established. The Society of Friends applied for and received permission to use part of North Main Street market as a soup kitchen. Within hours of opening, 400 gallons had been handed out. From then, 3,000 pints of soup were distributed locally each day. By mid-December, the Cork Relief Committee had established the Southern and Central Soup Depot Committee, which quickly set up five soup kitchens in the city.

A new workhouse opened on the Douglas Road and initially 3,000 inmates and 4,256 non-residents were admitted. By mid-October 1846 the number of workhouse inmates had climbed to over 3,500, with 11,633 non-residents; 500 were admitted in one week alone. The level of overcrowding was not confined to the living. A report in the *Southern Reporter* stated that seventy bodies remained unburied in the workhouse. The graveyards of the inner city had simply run out of space. Fr Mathew suggested to the Board that it purchase ground for burials. Land was acquired from George Carr, a workhouse official, on the road between Douglas and Carrigaline. Christened All Saints Cemetery, it was more commonly known as the Graveyard of the Unknown as headstones were rare.

n April 1847 a second report appeared, this time in the *Cork Constitution,* condemning the state of the cemetery. Dogs had been witnessed digging up human remains from shallow pits. According to the editorial, in one gruesome incident a dog had carried human remains into the house of a man named Reardon. The Board of Guardians of the Workhouse chose to ignore the criticisms, but further reports of malpractice were printed. On 8 July 1847 an application was made at Douglas Petty Sessions, a local court, to prevent further burials taking place. Several witnesses appeared for the prosecution and described a strong, unpleasant odour in the graveyard. They also described scenes of bodies half-buried in pits that were left uncovered overnight. Carr was prosecuted and lost his contract, but soon regained it when no suitable plots of land became available.

Today All Saints Cemetery is completely overgrown and all that remains to be seen is the encompassing wall, entrance gate, a large commemorative plaque for the Famine victims and a twentieth-century cross erected in the 1950s by Booney Sorensen, a taxi driver who acted as caretaker of the site for many years. The cross was originally lit up at night, but that practice was discontinued in 1979.

As the spring of 1847 progressed, fever and malnutrition were rampant in the lanes and alleys of the city as the death toll continued to rise. The country was on its knees and no help was forthcoming. Then, just as people had lost all hope, the summer of 1848 brought with it a healthy potato harvest.

During the Famine and after, a new problem emerged: emigration. As one of the principal ports for the emigrants, Cork witnessed huge numbers of people boarding ships to America, Australia and Britain. The exodus was unprecedented and had a huge effect on the country, socially and psychologically. Between 1851 and 1871 approximately 266,000 people departed from Cork Harbour. An excellent heritage centre at Cobh pays tribute to the *émigrés*.

The Divided City

As the city moved into the late nineteenth century, it was still facing huge social problems. It was estimated at the time that 11,000 families were living in slum conditions. The three most overcrowded parishes were Holy Trinity, St Paul's and St Peter's. Sanitary facilities

Constructed in 1886, the seventy-six houses of Madden's Buildings were built in Blackpool, on the site of the old cattle market. This was one of several attempts by Cork Corporation to improve the standard of housing in the city.

were completely inadequate, resulting in disease and death. In 1874 and 1878 the Public Health Act (Ireland) was passed, making Cork Corporation an urban sanitary authority. Water supply and sewage disposal were the first items on their agenda.

There were several free public schools which the poor could attend. The most notable was the Christian Brothers-run North Monastery, with rooms at Blarney Street and Sullivan's Quay. There was also the South Presentation Monastery, which likewise had two schools – Lancastrian School and Greenmount School, both established in the 1860s. For girls, there were classes in reading and writing at the North and South Presentation convents and at St Marie's of the Isle.

Late Georgian Cork displays the fine architecture and decorative features of the period.

The lower and middle classes had always lived in different parts of Cork, and this division was maintained in the late nineteenth century. After the Famine, the wealthier citizens began to build new houses to the west of the old medieval core, in the area of Mayoralty House (now Mercy Hospital), and in the city's hinterland, particularly in Montenotte. The type of house being built had changed since the early decades of the 1800s. In 1824, houses of the middle classes were large, detached and expensive. In 1853, they built mostly modest terraced housing. The best examples are found at Summerhill north and in the area around St Luke's Church.

The middle classes were privileged in their access to education, too. Private schools were serious educational establishments, usually conducted in former private residences. Many were located in areas accessible only by horse and carriage, emphasising their élite status. The fees for private schools were high, on average thirty guineas per annum. Consequently, neither skilled nor unskilled workers could afford to educate their children privately.

In the boys' schools, commercial subjects were taught along with science subjects, such as engineering, geometry, arithmetic, trigonometry and algebra. Some schools even offered classes in astronomy and mapping. English, Greek, Latin and Hebrew were the standard subjects, along with history and geography. In accordance with the mores of the day, girls were taught subjects associated with their future roles as housewives and ladies. They studied ornamental work, dancing and languages. French, German and Italian were taught in several girls' schools.

The middle class played a leading role in promoting cultural societies in the city. In the early nineteenth century, Cork was known as the 'Athens of Ireland'. This reputation was secured by the work of a group of internationally renowned Cork artists, including the artist Daniel Maclise, sculptor John Hogan, and writers William Maginn, Francis Mahony, Crofton Croker and Samuel Carter Hall.

The Royal Cork Institution (1803) was instrumental in bringing such people together. Based in the eighteenth-century custom house, it pioneered adult education in disciplines such as science, natural history and botany. The institution collected a library of specialised books for the benefit of its members. The Cuverian Society (1853) had twenty-one members who met regularly to discuss science, literature and fine art. The Cork Literary and Scientific Society (1834) promoted discussion on science subjects. The more popular subjects included zoology, botany, geology, astronomy, meteorology and electricity. In 1850 it had 4,000 members, primarily drawn from the gentry, the clergy and the professional class.

For the wealthy, the theatre also provided a stimulating diversion. There were two main theatres – the Victoria Theatre on Cook Street and the Theatre Royal on Mary Street. Operas, particularly Italian operas, and theatrical presentations were frequent, with over forty operas and 100 plays performed in Cork between 1850 and 1860 by both local and visiting companies. There was also a circus area in Mary Street used for equestrian displays and other exhibitions.

From 1855 onwards, a new building called the Athenaeum (now Cork Opera House) became the fashionable venue for social events. The admission fee to the inaugural ball at the Athenaeum cost £1, or 5% of a working man's yearly wage. Balls were also held in one of the city's principal hotels, the Imperial Hotel, or the Clarence Hotel as it was known then.

The Theatre Royal, now the General Post Office on Oliver Plunkett Street, was frequented by the rich who enjoyed operatic and dramatic performances there.

Economics and Politics

A National Exhibition was held in 1852 in an attempt to promote industry in Cork. This was in response to a distinct decline in the economic fortunes of the city. The early nineteenth century had seen Blackpool emerge as a centre of industry, but by the late 1800s this area too was in decline due to competing foreign markets. Blackpool was renowned for its tanyards. In 1845, sixty tanyards existed here, but by the closing decade of the 1800s only sixteen remained. This was due largely to the introduction of cheap, machine-made boots and shoes from abroad. Indeed, the only profitable commodities at the time for Cork were corn and wool. In 1883, the city possessed twelve woollen factories, with the most profitable mills located at Donnybrook, in Douglas.

The nineteenth century was important in terms of the expansion of the city. Bridges, railways and much new housing was built. Four principal bridges spanned the two channels of the River Lee – South Gate, North Gate, St Patrick's Bridge and George IV Bridge – but now many new bridges were added. Wellington Bridge was opened in 1830. St Patrick's Bridge was rebuilt in 1861, St Vincent's Bridge in 1875, and a Victorian-style cast-iron North Gate Bridge was built in 1863. (The present-day North Gate Bridge was opened in 1961 on the same site.) On the south channel, County Gaol Bridge was opened in 1834; University Bridge in 1849; Parliament Bridge in 1806 and

The *SS Sabrina* leaving Cork. In the nineteenth century steamships were a popular form of transport from the port of Cork to America and Britain.

Anglesea Bridge in 1830, named after the Marquis of Anglesea who lived in the city. It had to be replaced in 1882 after a ship got stuck between the two secure parts of the bridge and held up traffic for days until it could finally be freed. Anglesea Bridge was later renamed Parnell Bridge, after Charles Stewart Parnell. Railways such as the Cork–Blackrock–Passage railway, or Cork Muskerry Light Railway provided access to the city and countryside. The service was improved and expanded when Glanmire (now Kent) Station opened in 1893. In the city, electric trams operated between 1898 and 1932.

Steamships increasingly became the common mode of transport for foreign travel. The City of Cork Steamship Company was established in 1843 under the direction of Ebenezer Pike. It was founded on the former site of the St George Steampacket Company. Neither of these companies built ships, instead they bought older steamships as well as commissioning new ones.

Perhaps the most famous steamship acquired was *Sirius*. The ship was named after the dog star Sirius and sported a canine figurehead. On 28 March 1838 it was the first passenger steamship to make the voyage from Europe to America, from London via Cork to New York.

Sirius made two further transatlantic voyages before it was bought by the Cork Steamship Company and employed in the Glasgow–Dublin–Cork service. Then its fortunes changed. On the evening of 15 June 1847, *en route* from Dublin to Cork with a general cargo and forty passengers, *Sirius* encountered dense fog and went onto the rocks at Ballycotton Bay. Twelve passengers and two seamen were drowned when one of the launch boats capsized. The rest of the passengers and crew were rescued.

The structure of local politics changed completely in the post-Famine period. In 1850 the Municipal Corporations Act ended the Protestant community's absolute control over municipalities. Religion became a minor factor in being elected to Cork Corporation. The key requirements now were wealth and class.

After Daniel O'Connell's death in May 1847, a new group emerged to fight for Home Rule. The Young Irelanders proposed that on the question of national identity, Protestants and Catholics could stand united. Led by Thomas Davis, they argued that the Act of Union had failed and had been detrimental to Irish society, denying personal liberties and creating widespread poverty.

In the early 1850s the Young Irelanders formed the Irish Tenant League, which aimed to secure fair rent, fixity of tenure and freedom for the tenant to sell his interest in his holding. Their agenda received much support. However, the party was split by anti-constitutionalism and by the question of using physical force to achieve their goals. As a result, it failed to win seats in the Westminster Parliament in 1852 and the party quickly disintegrated.

A number of its members established a new organisation known as the Irish Republican Brotherhood (IRB), which was founded in Dublin and New York in 1858. The IRB believed that Britain would never concede independence without the use of physical force. By 1867, thousands had enrolled and were preparing for action.

In the late 1850s and 1860s, the IRB gained much support in Cork. Two men in particular were in the vanguard of the movement: Brian Dillon (1830–72) and Jeremiah O'Donovan Rossa (1831–1915). Dillon is reputed to have personally drilled recruits in the city. He was imprisoned in 1866 for ten years for republican activities, but was released after five years on health grounds. On his return to Cork, he received massive public support but died a few months later. In February 1908, a commemorative plaque was unveiled at Dillon's Cross, and later a Celtic cross was erected at nearby Rathcooney.

O'Donovan Rossa was tried in 1865 and sentenced to lifelong penal servitude. He was released in 1871 but expelled from Ireland. He subsequently emigrated to America and became involved in the Fenian movement there. He founded a weekly newspaper in New York called *United Ireland* and worked tirelessly for the Irish cause until his death on Staten Island in July 1915.

All was not doom and gloom in the city, however. The latter half of the 1800s saw the present townscape emerge. In terms of architecture, the 1850s and 1860s saw a new generation of ornate buildings gracing the city's streets. This applied especially to church architecture. The Protestant Cathedral of St FinBarre (foundation stone laid in 1865) and SS. Mary and Anne's North Chapel (foundation stone laid in 1869) were to become grand cathedrals. SS Peter and Paul's Church was reconstructed, and the foundation stone of Trinity Presbyterian Church was laid in 1861.

Early Twentieth-century Cork

The new century witnessed the consolidation of Ireland's sense of identity, and a renewed vigour for the policy of Home Rule. Queen Victoria's visit to Ireland in April 1900 did not occasion the same level of adulation seen on previous Royal visits. The main effect of the Royal visit on Cork was that the title for Cork's first citizen was changed to Lord Mayor. Daniel J Hegarty had the honour of becoming the city's first Lord Mayor.

There was also a new-found pride in Irish culture, promoted earnestly by organisations such as the GAA and Conradh na Gaeilge. In politics, this sense of pride in national identity was reflected in the work of the Irish Parliamentary Party (IPP), which strove to secure Home Rule. First Charles Stewart Parnell, then John Redmond led their MPs in Westminster and pursued a satisfactory answer to the Irish Question.

In 1914 the British Prime Minister Herbert Asquith passed the Government of Ireland Act, which made provision for Ulster Unionist concerns regarding Home Rule. The diplomatic work was interrupted by the outbreak of war. Many Corkmen pledged their allegiance to the allied cause against Germany and many were rewarded on their return with housing in the suburbs. Veterans' houses were built at Haig Gardens (Boreenamanna Road), Fair Hill (Blackpool) and Whitethorn (Douglas). All were State-supported with a minimum of private investment and all are still occupied.

After the war the nationalists were more focused than ever on Home Rule, believing a republic could be achieved quickly through revolution rather than through negotiation. On Easter Monday, 24 April 1916 a group of volunteers left Liberty Hall in Dublin and marched on the General Post Office, intending to take the city. The Rising failed, but the fight for Irish freedom had just begun.

Two men played a pivotal role in the drive for Irish independence: Eamon de Valera, who was born and raised in Limerick, and Michael Collins, who was born and raised in Clonakilty, County Cork. Together they made Sinn Féin a potent force in Anglo-Irish politics. In 1919, members of Sinn Féin, including de Valera and Collins, set up their own parliament, Dáil Éireann, which was completely opposed by the British authorities. The new government of the Republic established the Irish Republican Army (IRA) to protect the fledgling State. The War of Independence had begun.

This was a dark time for the country, a time when Cork lived up to its rebel name. The city's uncompromising stance was epitomised by two men: Tomás MacCurtain and Terence MacSwiney. Both are immortalised in sculptures in the grounds of City Hall. Mac-Curtain was born in Bally-knockane in Mallow, County

Terence MacSwiney

LORD MAYOR OF CORK, DIED A MARTYR FOR HIS COUNTRY OCTOBER 25TH, 1920 AFTER A HUNGERSTRIKE LASTING 74 DAYS FIGHTING FOR IRELAND'S FREEDOM.

Terence MacSwiney, Lord Mayor of Cork in 1920 and a key figure in the War of Independence.

Cork. In 1907 he contributed to the National Council of Sinn Féin, and in the same year he became a member of the IRB. He enlisted as an Irish Volunteer in late 1913 and was periodically imprisoned in various English jails. In early 1920 he was elected Sinn Féin council-lor for Cork Northwest, and on 20 January 1920 he became Lord Mayor of Cork.

MacSwiney also took an active part in the Irish Volunteers, but he promoted the cause through the written word as well. Between 1910 and 1914 he wrote five plays, two of which were in verse. One of his greatest works, *The Principles of Freedom,* appeared in serial form in a Dublin monthly newspaper, *Irish Freedom.*

Early on the morning of 20 March 1920, Lord Mayor Tomás Mac-Curtain was found murdered at his home. MacSwiney claimed that the execution had been carried out by the Royal Irish Constabulary (RIC), under the direction of the British government. There was huge public outcry. MacSwiney was re-arrested and transported to Brixton Prison where he died on 25 October 1920 after a hunger strike lasting seventy-four days.

In response to IRA activities in Cork and in the country as a whole, the British government increased the number of men serving in the RIC, recruiting the infamous Black and Tans to swell the ranks. The total number in the RIC was now about 40,000, whilst the IRA numbered 5,000 men. Thus, more often than not the IRA employed hit-and-run tactics. On 28 November 1920, a famous incident involv-ing the British auxiliaries and the IRA occurred near Cork. The 'Flying Column' – a division of the West Cork IRA – ambushed a police patrol near the village of Kilmichael, just south of Macroom. Twenty British soldiers were killed. In West Cork and across the country, Kilmichael became a celebrated rebel victory.

In December 1920, six IRA men ambushed a troupe of auxiliaries within a hundred metres of the central military barracks near Dillon's Cross. In retaliation, the Black and Tans set alight many buildings in the city. The fires spread rapidly and soon most of the eastern side of St Patrick's Street was blazing. City Hall and Carnegie Library were gutted, and large tranches of Cork's public and historic records were destroyed forever.

In 1921 delegates from Dáil Éireann went to Britain to negotiate a peace treaty. The controversial treaty was not welcomed by all, but it was passed nonetheless. Eamon de Valera resigned as president of the Irish Republic; Michael Collins was appointed chairman of the provisional government. A Civil War was inevitable. Former comrades became sworn enemies and the country was engulfed in a tide of violence. In August 1922, Collins was killed at an ambush at Béal na mBláth, near Crookstown in County Cork. As a tribute to him, Victoria Barracks was renamed Collins Barracks. He is also commemorated by a beautifully sculpted bust located in the grounds of Fitzgerald's Park. He was buried in Glasnevin Cemetery, Dublin.

Conditions in Cork were difficult after the War of Independence. Although the 1920s saw the opening of a huge Ford car factory in Cork, business was not booming in general. The lull of the late nineteenth century continued into the twentieth century and in 1902 the Corporation and Lord Mayor Edward Fitzgerald decided to organise an international exhibition to highlight what the city had to offer to investors. The exhibition was held on the grounds of what is now the Mardyke. After the exhibition ended, the purpose-built buildings were taken down and a public park was laid out and named Fitzgerald's Park in honour of the Lord Mayor.

The issue of the provision of decent social housing had yet to be satisfactorily resolved. A survey published by the Cork Town Planning Association revealed that 12,850 houses were occupied by 15,469 families. Nearly 9,000 families were still living in tenements. The suggested improvements involved re-housing on a massive scale. The Civic Survey outlined that 16,000 people would have to be re-housed. Subsequently, in 1905, 1906 and 1907 more Local Authority houses were built: Sutton's Buildings (46 houses), Barrett's Buildings (73 houses), Kelleher Buildings (50 houses). This was followed later by MacCurtain Villas in 1922 (76 houses), French's Villas in 1923 (30 houses) and MacSwiney's Villas in 1923 (40 houses). All are still lived in.

In the southern suburbs the area of Turner's Cross was quickly built up with Corporation housing, and as a result the area became a parish in 1927. Between 1928 and 1932 a new church, Christ the King, was built here. Another area of rapid development was nearby Ballinlough. It was chosen as a site for Local Authority housing and between 1936 and 1942 seven estates were built here. Between 1934 and 1944, a total of 1,876 houses were built by the Corporation and some 10,800 people were relocated.

Unfortunately, the Second World War forced all development to be curtailed and plunged the city into further economic decline.

New houses in Gurranabraher, 17 March 1934. Note the contrast between the old and the new presented by the adjacent thatched cottage, which had been the standard accommodation of the poor in the previous century.

The Late Twentieth-century and Beyond

By the 1950s a shortage of land for new housing estates meant more city suburbs, such as Ballyphehane (southside) and Farranree (northside), were built up. Nearly, 1,000 houses were constructed in Ballyphehane alone between 1948 and 1960. The Corporation also bought up land in the city's southern suburbs, such as the Lough. Much of this land was used as market gardens to supply the stalls at Coal Quay and the English Market. On the northside of the city, Churchfield was developed. Such was the extent of building in the suburbs that in 1955 the Corporation decided to recognise the development outside the city boundary and, in conjunction with the County Council, extended the municipal boundary by 856 acres.

The 1950s was also the time of one of the city's most determined religious leaders, Bishop Cornelius Lucey, who was appointed Bishop of Cork and Ross in 1954. He will be remembered principally for his dedication in establishing church-building schemes in Cork, resulting in the building of the Church of the Ascension, Gurranabraher (1955); the Church of the Assumption, Ballyphehane, (1956); the Church of the Resurrection, Farranree (1958); the Church of the Descent of the Holy Spirit, Dennehy's Cross (1960); and the Church of the Way of the Cross, Togher (1972). Today, the city's central park is named after Bishop Lucey. The impressive entrance gates are those of the city's nineteenth-century corn market, a site now occupied by City Hall. Within the park, sections of the medieval town wall can be seen.

This period also witnessed the rise to power of one of Cork's favourite sons, Jack Lynch. Born in 1917, Lynch was a gifted sportsman. In the 1940s he played on the Cork All-Ireland minor and senior football teams, winning several All Ireland medals. His second passion was politics and in 1966 he succeeded Seán Lemass to become Taoiseach. He was a leading figure in the negotiating team that signed the Treaty of Accession to the EEC – a move that initiated Ireland's economic recovery and Celtic Tiger days.

In the early 1960s, Cork was consolidating its position as the southern capital of Ireland. At the same time, an innovative national development strategy was devised to stimulate industrial growth and spatial redistribution by means of a new policy of free

Ornate fountain in Bishop Lucey Park, commemorating Cork's 800th anniversary in 1985. Each of the eight swans represents a century of the town's history.

In 1994 the Cork Historic Centre Action Plan converted the medieval St Peter's Church for use as the Cork Vision Centre.

trade and foreign investment. Cork's existing industrial base, its urban infrastructures, the large labour force and ideal port facilities provided the context for significant growth in its manufacturing base. Within the county borough, chemical and engineering sectors thrived, especially at Ringaskiddy. Today, multinational companies such as Pfizers, ADM and Smith-Kline Beecham are still based in Cork.

Cork Airport opened in 1961 and was Ireland's third airport after Shannon and Dublin. It helped to sell Cork as a base for multinationals. The arrival of new manufacturing industries in Cork meant an increase in the number of people living in the city. The population in 1961 was 115,689 and this escalated by nearly 10,000 to 125,283 in 1966. As a result, in 1965 the city boundary expanded to the north and south yet again. This time an area of 6,250 acres was encompassed. Since then the city boundary has remained fixed, comprising an area of approximately thirty-nine square kilometres.

In 1967 the first flats were built in the city, at Blackpool. The following year Cork Corporation proposed its first development plan. As a result, major housing schemes were built at Knocknaheeny (northside), Mayfield (northside), Mahon (northside) and Togher (southside), and new industrial estates such as Hollymount in Hollyhill (northside) were constructed.

The early 1970s saw the population of Cork City rise by a further 10,000 people. In 1978 a coherent plan was published by the Land Utilisation and Transport Study (LUTS), and nearly all those proposals have been realised. For example, a downstream crossing was proposed and it opened in May 1998 at the Lee Tunnel, or to give it its official title, the Jack Lynch Tunnel. These new routeways have dramatically altered the approaches to the city. LUTS also encouraged the construction of more bridges, including Donovan's Bridge (1900), Brian Ború Bridge (1915), Trinity Footbridge (1977), Eamon de Valera Bridge (1984), Michael Collins Bridge (1984) and Nano Nagle Footbridge (1985). New bridges on the north channel include Clontarf Bridge (1915), Daly's Bridge (1926) and Christy Ring Bridge (1985).

In the late 1970s and early 1980s new housing developments appeared at the Commons, Ballyvolane, Lota, Montenotte, Kilbarry and Mahon. In the 1970s three institutions opened in the Wilton–Bishopstown area: the Regional Technical College (1978), now the Cork Institute of Technology; Cork Regional Hospital (1979), now Cork University Hospital; and regional offices of the Industrial Development Authority (IDA).

Alongside the rush to expand and change is the equally important drive to conserve and retain. The Cork Historic Centre Action Plan aimed to promote business activity, refurbish properties and

Placename plaques recalling the various trades that existed in the early life of the town can be seen on North Main Street's pavements.

increase residential use of the city centre. North Main Street was chosen as the primary focus and a number of initiatives were completed, including a 'living-over-the-shop' scheme facilitated by the building of apartments over shops. Other heritage projects included a large-scale archaeological dig prior to the construction of North Main Street Shopping Centre, the restoration of eighteenth-century houses at Fenn's Quay and the restoration of St Peter's Church, formerly one of the medieval churches within the walled town. St Peter's and the houses at Fenn's Quay are some of over 450 protected historical buildings in the city today.

Twenty-first-century architecture has also found a place in Cork. The façades of the Cork Opera House and Gate Cinema are two noteworthy examples. A complete overhaul of St Patrick's Street is currently underway. Rebuilt to the designs of Spanish architect Beth Gali, it will be a retail and business quarter worthy of a European regional capital. Furthermore, the Cork Docklands Project is also working on a new urban quarter.

Cork as European City of Culture

The twenty-first century will see Cork become European City of Culture 2005. A huge boon to the life of the city, the award recognises Cork's long and illustrious cultural history. Cork Opera House is the only purpose-built opera house in the Republic. The Everyman Palace, the Cork Arts Theatre, the Granary and the Triskel Arts Centre are but a few of the fine performance venues in the city. Other cultural venues of note include the Kino Cinema on Washington Street and the Firkin Crane, a dance centre at Shandon.

For the best part of a century, the Crawford School of Art served both as an art school and as a public gallery. Today the college is housed in a separate building near St FinBarre's Cathedral, and the original site is occupied by the internationally acclaimed Crawford Municipal Art Gallery. The galleries have been extended and the collection includes the work of James Barry, Nathaniel Grogan, Walter Osborne, Paul Henry, Jack B Yeats, Harry Clarke and Sean Keating.

There are a number of thriving arts organisations in the city, of national and international significance, including the brand new arts facility at Wandesford Quay, the National Sculpture Factory and the

Cork's reputation as a city of culture has been greatly enhanced by the work of the Opera House (*above*) and the Crawford Municipal Art Gallery in Emmet Place.

Triskel Arts Centre, which acts as a public 'art laboratory' for developing and presenting new and challenging work across the arts.

Cork has a distinguished literary tradition too, and among its most famous writers are Daniel Corkery, Seán Ó Faoláin and Frank O'Connor. It has also spawned some of the finest musicians in Ireland, like Sean Ó Riada, Aloysius Fleischmann and Rory Gallagher. One of the city's best-known artists is Seamus Murphy, a sculptor whose work can be seen in various locations around the city.

Cork also has a strong connection with ballet. Joan Denise Moriarty was born in Cork in the 1920s. She trained in London and Paris to become a professional dancer, but her dream was shattered by illness. In 1941 she returned to Cork and opened a ballet school on St

Patrick's Street, establishing the Cork Ballet Group (later the Cork Ballet Company). In 1959, Moriarty founded the Irish Theatre Ballet, which toured nationwide, but it was forced to close after only five years due to financial difficulties. At this time, the Irish government allocated funds for the Irish National Ballet to be established.

Cork has long been identified as a festival city. Annual festivals include the Cork International Choral Festival in April, which has taken place since 1954. The Cork International Film Festival takes place every October, while the Guinness Jazz Festival is a highlight of the October bank-holiday weekend. Other festivals include the Cork Arts Festival, the Midsummer Arts Festival, Fringe Theatre Festival, Cork Folk Festival, as well as a literary festival celebrating the work of Frank O'Connor.

Cork Institute of Technology (CIT) is one of the largest and oldest technological education centres in Ireland. The CIT also hosts an annual arts festival, which has developed into a citywide event. At its debut in 1993, Rory Gallagher played a showcase gig in what was to be his last Irish concert. Paul Street Plaza has since been renamed Rory Gallagher Place and a commemorative sculpture by Geraldine Creedon has been placed there in his memory.

As a city on the very edge of western Europe, Cork has benefitted from an anthology of influences. It has a culture that is distinct. One can walk down St Patrick's Street and still hear the cries of the 'Echo boys' while admiring innovative twenty-first-century architecture. Cork will face challenges and unique opportunities to forge links between the arts, cultural, heritage, sporting, educational, public service, tourism and business communities. As the City of Culture programme suggests, the future will offer:

> '... the fresh water of culture with song, dance, paint-
> ing, film, community, sport, food and drink; a quality
> of life with the noises and marks made by people and
> the imprint of European laughter, good humour and
> converging hopes; a sense of welcome with crowds
> converging and ideas debated; and a sense of human
> value, a pilgrimage and mighty street party – all deliv-
> ered within a safe harbour.'

Panoramic view of Cork city centre, taken from the northern suburbs of Churchfield.
Note the tower of Shandon at the centre of the picture.

Present-day City Hall was opened in 1936 by Eamon de Valera.
The previous structure had been destroyed by the Black and Tans in 1920.

The majestic spires of St FinBarre's Cathedral.

Right: A collection of medieval artefacts held in the Cork Public Museum.

George Richard Pain's masterpiece, Holy Trinity Church, the foundation stone of which was laid in 1832.

Left: The pillars of the entrance to the Butter Market, overshadowed by St Anne's Church, Shandon.

Below: A taste of Cork – inside the English Market, which has been in operation since 1788.

The superb façade of Christ the King Church in Turner's Cross, which opened in 1932. It is based on a church in Chicago, designed by Barry Byrne.

Left: An unusual view of the Golden Angel of St FinBarre's Cathedral, when it was placed on the ground during recent renovations. It was a gift from the architect of the cathedral, William Burges, to the Protestant parish of St FinBarre's.

Below: The Quadrangle at UCC, designed by Sir Thomas Deane and opened in 1849 as Queen's College, Cork.

Above: Daly's Bridge, affectionately known as the Shaky Bridge,
was opened in 1927. James Daly
was a butter merchant in the city.

Right: Henry T Ford established a
car factory in Cork in 1920. The
production plant was built on the
city's nineteenth-century public
park, next to the Marina.

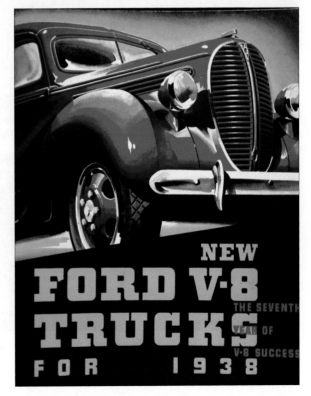

NEW
FORD V-8
TRUCKS
FOR   1938
THE SEVENTH
YEAR OF
V-8 SUCCESS

St Anthony's Shrine, housed in St Francis Church on Liberty Street.

The tower of St Peter's Church, now the home of the Cork Vision Centre.
There has been a church on this site since 1199.

Above: Cork is known as a city of colour, and façades such as this are the reason why. Named after the Grand Circle in the Opera House, inside there is an illustrated history of that building.

Left: Twenty-first-century architecture at the Gate Cinema, at North Gate Bridge.

Above: The Drunken Faun (1826), sculpted by John Hogan and presented to the Royal Cork Institution by WH Crawford. It is on display in the Crawford Municipal Art Gallery.

Above: Nineteenth-century golden façade on Grand Parade, opposite Berwick Fountain.

The Crawford Municipal Art Gallery boasts a fine mix of old and modern art. This vibrant stained-glass window illuminates the stairway to the first floor.

Right: Bishop Lucey Park, overlooked by Christ Church, is a favourite spot to sit and watch the crowds go by in summer.

Below: The elegant façade of St Mary's Dominican Church, which dominates Pope's Quay. The spire of Shandon is visible to the left.

St Francis Church on Liberty Street. Built in 1953, this church replaced an older nineteenth-century Franciscan church known as Broad Lane Church.

Above: The entrance to Honan Chapel, UCC, designed by James F McMullen.

Above: St Vincent's Church, Sunday's Well, designed by Sir John Benson for the Vincentian Fathers. Building work commenced in 1851 and was completed in 1856.

Left: The Waterworks lie west of Thomas Davis Bridge. Designed by Sir John Benson, it was built in 1888.

Below: The many faces of the Crawford Municipal Art Gallery: one side, on Half Moon Street, is a modern façade, built in the late twentieth century; next is a nineteenth-century entrance to what was the Crawford School of Art; and finally, the Emmet Place frontage bears fine eighteenth-century architectural details as it was the entrance to the custom house, built in 1720.

GUIDE TO THE HISTORIC CITY

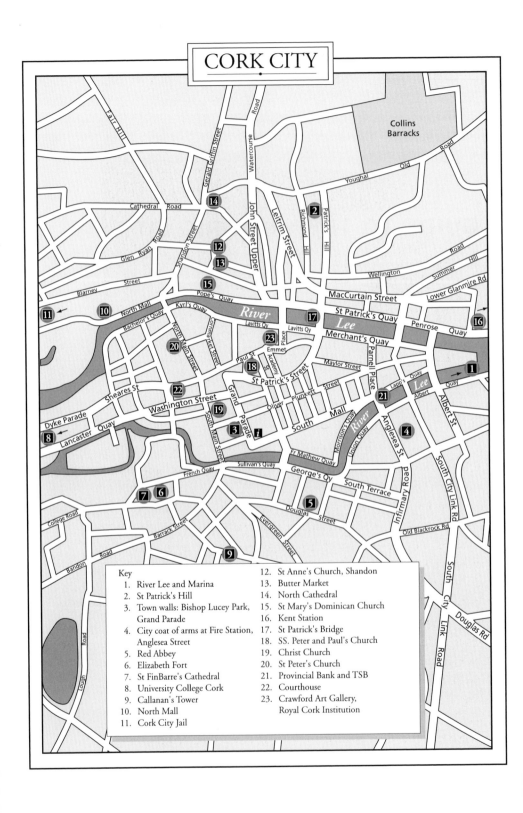

CORK CITY

Key

1. River Lee and Marina
2. St Patrick's Hill
3. Town walls: Bishop Lucey Park, Grand Parade
4. City coat of arms at Fire Station, Anglesea Street
5. Red Abbey
6. Elizabeth Fort
7. St FinBarre's Cathedral
8. University College Cork
9. Callanan's Tower
10. North Mall
11. Cork City Jail
12. St Anne's Church, Shandon
13. Butter Market
14. North Cathedral
15. St Mary's Dominican Church
16. Kent Station
17. St Patrick's Bridge
18. SS. Peter and Paul's Church
19. Christ Church
20. St Peter's Church
21. Provincial Bank and TSB
22. Courthouse
23. Crawford Art Gallery, Royal Cork Institution

RIVER LEE AND MARINA

A sweeping view of the Lower Road with the Marina in the background, taken in the 1920s. The river is a hive of activity, the focal point of the city.

On his visit to Cork in the 1850s, antiquary Byron Cody wrote that the River Lee 'flows through one of the most beautiful and fertile plains of the sunny south, its course lies between scenes of sylvan but changeful loveliness; through pleasant vales, shaded by scattered clumps of trees; by green hills and lawny uplands, which laugh back the smiles of heaven, on which groups of cattle pasture or ruminate; past stately villas with spreading lawns and by fields of rich pasturage and vivid greenness.'

Nowadays, of course, the environs of the Lee are not quite so idyllic. The river wends it way through a busy city, past buildings both old and modern. It begins its long journey in the Shehy Mountains in West Cork and makes a seventy-kilometre journey to Cork Harbour through an array of landscapes.

The origin of the name 'Lee' is uncertain. Legend attributes it to a group known as the Milesians, who arrived in Ireland in the prehistoric period. The Milesians are said to have acquired land in southern Munster, lands they named Corca Luighe, or Cork of the Lee, after Luighe, son of Ith.

The river has long been the focal point of the city's development and was a key factor in its growth, providing transport and energy. In the eighteenth century, it provided water for the city's new canals. In the closing decades of the century, the river provided the impetus for the establishing of several breweries and distilleries. One famous Cork brewery, the River Lee Porter Brewery, established in 1796, was operated by water-powered machinery. In 1813 the brewery was bought by William Beamish and William Crawford who used the site as a storage area for their malting operation, hence its alternative name, the Lee Maltings. In the late 1800s a new storehouse was opened adjacent to the South Mall and the Porter site was closed. In recent years, the site has been bought by UCC and has been entirely modernised for the college's requirements.

In the eighteenth and early nineteenth centuries, the city's upper classes built their residences, gardens and plantations overlooking the river and harbour. Fine examples include *Lotamore House* in Mayfield, now a guest house, and the Ursuline Convent in Blackrock, originally a mansion constructed in 1720 by Christopher Tuckey, a city merchant. The riverside dwellers paid ferrymen to punt them across the river. As the city developed and the marshes were reclaimed, the livelihood of these gentlemen was jeopardised and finally rendered defunct by the construction of various bridges.

As a city built on a series of marshy islands where the river meets the tide, flooding is a common occurrence in Cork. In November 1853 a devastating flood washed over the city, wiping out St Patrick's Bridge and North Gate Bridge. The *Illustrated London News* described the deluge:

> 'The rains of Monday and Tuesday of that faithful week, as indicated by the gauge kept at the Royal Cork Institution of Mr. Humphrey's amounted to a total of 2 ½ inches. However, five inches had fallen in the preceding fortnight. This coupled with a new moon, a rising tide of just over 20 feet along with hurricane conditions, which blew from the south-east, caused the elevation of the water levels in the city's channels. As a result, on Tuesday evening, water started to rise at four o'clock and in the space of a half an hour, the whole flat of the city inundated ...'

One area in particular brings the walker back to another age. The Marina is a walkway that was built in the Victorian age and funded by Cork Corporation. It was designed to provide respite from the commercial centre of the city. The original walkway, constructed in the 1780s, was a dock called the Navigation Wall, which was basically a narrow wall jutting out into the river. In the early nineteenth century, gravel and mud were dredged from the river to reclaim the adjacent slobland and create the popular Marina Walk. The walkway was lined with trees to shade and enclose the area. Eventually, after reclamation, a racecourse was opened in the vicinity in 1869, which lasted until the early 1920s when the Ford car factory was constructed on the site. The Marina is now home to the well-known Lee Rowing Club, which uses the river throughout the year.

A CITY OF HILLS AND VIEWS

Cork City is set in a valley, overlooked by a series of hills. Over the centuries, artists, travellers and antiquaries have tried to capture the unique topography of the place and the fine views it affords. The steepest and highest hill is St Patrick's Hill, towering above the city beyond St Patrick's Street. The climber is rewarded at the summit with a panoramic view of the city and its environs. There is a spectacular view of the whole city, especially of the northern suburbs at Blackpool, Gurranabraher, Knocknaheeny and Farranree. The river meanders through the scene, lazily intent on making its way to meet the waters of the Atlantic Ocean.

The view from the top has been reproduced in a variety of media through the ages. Famous examples include a sketch by historian Charles Smith in 1750, a painting by John Butt in the 1760s (now on display in the Crawford Municipal Art Gallery) and early nineteenth-century postcards. The early depictions illustrate the growth of Blackpool as an industrial hub, with its myriad chimneys confirming the presence of many tanneries and distilleries in the area.

St Anne's Church, Shandon, and its ornate steeple dominate all the images produced from the hilltop. The tower is symbolic of eighteenth-century expansion in Cork. The adjacent butter market, located off Shandon Street, remembers the golden age of trade and prosperity in the city. Tucked into the top corner of one of the early

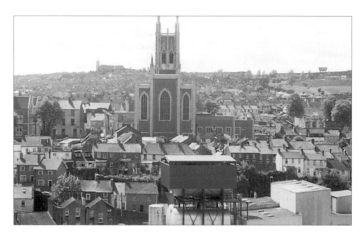

View from top of St Patrick's Hill, taking in the northwestern suburbs.
The North Cathedral dominates the centre of the photograph.

nineteenth-century photographs is a small cluster of farmed green
fields. This area was built over with housing estates in the early
1930s.

In former days St Patrick's Hill was a favourite spot for an afternoon stroll. Nowadays, it isn't frequented as much, but the City
Council (formerly Cork Corporation) is endeavouring to change that
by placing seating at the top and landscaping the whole area. It is
worth visiting for the unparalleled aerial view of the city and, of
course, the sense of achievement as one crests the summit.

THE TOWN WALLS

In 1984–85, Bishop Lucey Park was created to celebrate the 800th
anniversary of the granting of the first Royal charter to the citizens of
the walled town of Cork. By happy coincidence, whilst preparing the
ground for the park a section of the town wall was revealed. In general, much of the town wall survives beneath the modern street surface and in some places has been incorporated into the foundations
of existing buildings, in particular buildings on the Grand Parade. In
recent decades, it has also been the commonest archaeological feature to be discovered during development of the inner city, for example, whilst laying the foundations for Kyrl's Quay car park in 1994
sections of the wall were uncovered.

Initially created by the Anglo-Normans c.1180, the wall was extended and rebuilt by English colonists through subsequent centuries up until the Siege of Cork in 1690. The wall encompassed 1,500 metres in circumference and was a symbol of municipal power, giving the citizens a strong sense of security.

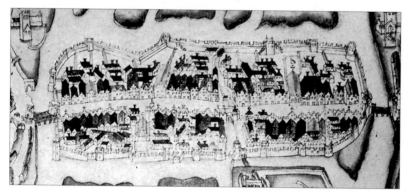

Map of Cork *c.*1601. It shows the extent of the walled area of the town. The site of Bishop Lucey Park is at the bottom left of the walled area.

Examination of the exposed wall by archaeologists suggests that it was approximately eight to ten metres high, two to three metres wide at the base and one metre wide at the top. It generally comprised boulders and compacted gravel and clay and exhibited evidence of rebuilding and repairing during its lifespan, c.1180–1690, for example, drainage holes have been found at the base of excavated sections. The type of stone used in its construction was limestone and sandstone, both quarried locally. The stone was cut into irregular blocks and laid in random courses with their long axes lying horizontally. Mortar was found between these blocks and an analysis of it revealed that it was composed of crushed egg-shells and charcoal mixed in with gritty lime mortar.

In several of the excavated sections a feature called a batter was noticeable. In general, the term 'batter' is used to describe the sloping outwards of a wall at its base, in other words, the base of the wall is thicker than the top. The batter works on the principle of spreading the weight over a wider area, thereby providing better support for the whole structure. The outer and inner faces of the wall were dressed and putlog holes, or scaffolding holes, have been revealed in excavated sections. The *Pacata Hibernia* depiction of the walled town c.1585–1600 shows that crenellations or stepped-up battlements formed the top of the wall, along with a wall-walk.

COAT OF ARMS AND OFFICIAL INSIGNIA

A safe harbour for ships: the current city coat of arms can be seen at the entrance to Cork Public Museum. This inscribed stone was salvaged from City Hall in 1920 after it burnt down.

The arms of Cork City were officially registered by the chief herald on 23 August 1949 and are described as follows: 'On waves of the sea a ship three masts in full sail proper between towers gules upon rocks also proper each tower surmounted by a flag argent charged with a saltire of third.'

The current coat of arms comprises two battlemented towers with a medieval galleon sailing between them. The towers are said to represent King's and Queen's Castles, which operated the medieval portcullis gate that allowed ships to enter the interior dock of the walled town. The Latin motto reads: *Statio Bene Fida Carinis*, or 'a safe harbour for ships'. This was taken from the second book of *The Aeneid*, line 23, with *bene* substituted for Virgil's *male*.

In *An Olla Podrida* (Vol. 2), Richard Sainthill describes a Cork City seal attached to a document dated 15 October 1498. One side of the seal bore the three Lions of England, the other showed a castle with two towers. In one of the towers stood a man with a bow, and in the other a man in a pleading attitude blowing a trumpet. A bridge connected the two towers, beyond which a ship could be seen. A pen-and-ink sketch of the arms by Daniel Maclise taken from a stone at the old custom house, North Main Street, shows another variant. In this, a ship sails between two towers or castles, bearing a sailor in Elizabethan period dress and a bird on the rigging. This sketch can be seen in the Cork Public Museum.

The coat of arms can be seen in various places throughout the city. Perhaps the most elaborate of these representations is that on the entrance to the Cork Fire Station on Anglesea Street, and also the silver-painted piece located on the Lower Glanmire Road–Youghal dual carriageway.

The city also has other official insignia. In the days of the Anglo-Normans, the Corporation of Cork had jurisdiction over the harbour,

Mayoralty House was constructed in the mid- to late 1700s and served as the formal residence of the city's mayor. It was converted for use as Mercy Hospital in 1852 by the Sisters of Mercy.

and for centuries the mayor symbolically asserted his authority over the harbour by throwing a dart into the sea at a particular point. Established under a charter of Henry VII, dated 1 August 1500, the custom of 'throwing the dart' was carried out until the twentieth century, when it was discontinued. In recent years, however, it has been resurrected by Cork City Council and the Lord Mayor's office.

The gold collar of S.S. links still worn by the Lord Mayors of Cork is a very fine example of civic insignia. It is a replica of a silver collar of S.S given by Queen Elizabeth to Maurice Roche, Mayor of Cork, in 1511. The links of the S.S. are joined alternately by looped gold and enamelled cinquefoils. There are fifty-one links in all, terminating in a gold portcullis. Attached to the chain is a medallion bearing on the obverse the City arms, and on the reverse the following inscription: 'Cork, 9th June, 1787. The Right Worshipful Samuel Rowland, Esq., Mayor, was publicly invested by the Common Speaker, on behalf of the Commons, in open Court of D'Oyer Hundred with the Gold Chain, and immediately after the Mayor conferred the like Honor on the High Sheriffs, and lastly the Ceremony of investing the Mayor with this Pendant and Collar of S.S. was performed by a Deputation from the Council.'

In 1961 the Cork Jewellers' Association presented to the Corporation a gold medallion to be worn by mayoresses. Recently a second collar was commissioned for general use by the Lord Mayor, with the real collar being kept for formal occasions. This sterling silver chain of office consists of twenty S.S. links and ten knot links, with the Cork arms joined to the collar by a portcullis.

The original Cork guilds mace was made in 1696 by Cork goldsmith Robert Goble with chasing, or additional detail, by a Flemish immigrant goldsmith, Charles Begheagle. The mace is 91.4 centimetres long with an eight-sided head, each face bearing the arms of crafts in the following order: goldsmiths, pewters, founders, saddlers, glaziers and glass-founders, merchant tailors, tin-plate makers and tobacco-pipe makers. The stem has a central knob on which are carved four figures representing the cardinal virtues – Temperance, Justice, Fortitude and Prudence. The coat of arms of Cork appears on the base and the Royal arms of William and Mary on the top.

Cork City Council now possesses four maces, alike in form and workmanship but varying in size. They range in length from 83.8 centimetres to 91.4 centimetres. Engraved perpendicular lines divide the heads into four spaces and between these lines are inscribed the words: John Baldwin, Esqr., Mayor Horatio Townsend, Christopher Carlton Esqr., Shers. 1738. In the intervening spaces are inscribed: (1) The Royal arms within the Order of the Garter, and the letters G.I.I.R., indicating the reign of George II (1727–60); (2) the St George Cross (for England); (3) the Harp (for Ireland); and (4) the coat of arms of Cork City.

RED ABBEY

The central bell tower at the church of Red Abbey is a relic of the Anglo-Norman period and is one of the last remaining structures dating to the era of the walled town of Cork. Invited to the city by the Anglo-Normans, the Augustinians established an abbey here sometime between 1270 and 1288. The order would have been quite large, accommodating at least fifty monks. Our main source of information on the history of the abbey is Sir James Ware, an Elizabethan antiquary who recorded its history in *De Hibernia et Antiquitatibus Eius* (1658).

Red Abbey occupied an area now bounded by Dunbar Street, Margaret Street, Mary Street and Douglas Street. It was dedicated to the

The belfry of Red Abbey is all that remains of the medieval Augustinian monastery. It became known as Red Abbey because of the sandstone used in its construction.

Most Holy Trinity but had several names, which appear on various maps. For example, in a map of Cork in 1545 it was shown as St Austin's, while in 1610 it was marked as St Augustine's. The nearby neighbourhood of Friars' Walk in Turner's Cross indicates that the area was once used as a cloister garth, or walking area, and eighteenth-century maps of Cork do indeed show that the gardens belonged to the abbey.

During Henry VIII's suppression of monasteries in the 1540s, Royal surveyors visited Red Abbey accompanied by local jurors, namely Walter Galwey, John Skiddy, Richard Gould and Patrick Coppinger. They reported that the Augustinians had a church, gardens, including self-sufficient vegetable gardens, a cemetery, an old and new dormitory, cloister garth and other usual structures of a religious house. They also noted that salmon fishing was carried on nearby and that the friars possessed a half-share in a local watermill.

Henry VIII ordered the closure of Red Abbey and the Augustinians were forced to leave for a short time. It is known that they did remain in the local area and aimed to stay established. As soon as they were allowed, conventual life resumed at Red Abbey. Sometime between 1687 and 1690, Ignatius Gould, merchant and property-owner, bought a section of Red Abbey from the friars, while the rest of the complex was given to Othowell Hayes of Ballinlough in the southern suburbs of Cork, who owned a thatched cabin with half an acre of land in Coulin, on the south side of the abbey. The monks vacated the abbey at that point. In 1690 Red Abbey was used as a base by the English to fire cannon balls into the city during the Siege of Cork.

The next mention of the Augustinians in Cork came in March 1744 when a government report on *The State of Popery* described a new friary in existence in Fishamble Lane. Rocque's map of Cork in 1759 clearly shows the site of the friary. It is hidden amongst the network of lanes that existed in the old quarter. Fishamble Lane no longer exists, but it would have been located near present-day Liberty Street. The report stated that three Augustinian friars were residing at this friary: John Casey, Laurence O'Toole and Augustine Byrne.

On 20 November 1780 the foundation stone of a new Augustinian priory was laid on the corner of Washington Street and the Grand Parade. It was replaced by the present church during the Second World War. This last church is still used by the Augustinian order.

In the mid-eighteenth century, some of the buildings at Red Abbey were used as part of a sugar refinery. The refinery burnt down accidentally in December 1799. Following this, the friary buildings, with the exception of the tower, were taken down piecemeal. The tower is maintained by Cork City Council, to which the structure was donated in 1951 by the contemporary owners. The tower is approximately thirty metres high and is one of Cork's most important protected historic structures. It can no longer be climbed, but one can enjoy the medieval architecture on the lower arches and on the upper windows.

Three excavations have been completed at Red Abbey in the last twenty-five years. The first took place in May 1977 on a section to the west of the remaining tower, now an amenity square. Twenty-five skeletons were discovered; the burials were found to have taken place over a number of years. However, it is thought that these burials date to the post-seventeenth century. A single piece of medieval Saintonge pottery from France was found, along with seventeenth-, eighteenth- and nineteenth-century pottery sherds. Approximately 300 pieces of lead shot were also recorded, probably dating to the Siege of Cork. In April 1992 an excavation took place to the north of the tower. Here two medieval walls were discovered along with a medieval floor surface and associated pottery dating to the mid-thirteenth century. The third excavation took place in 2000 when more medieval walls were uncovered.

It has been alleged that there are vaults, or buried rooms, situated south of the tower, but this area has not yet been excavated. Sometime in the early 1800s, a restless horse on the grounds of a yard in Cove Street smashed its hoof through the ground. On investigation, the horse's owner, John Sisk, found underground passages with brick arches. A story told at the time relates that a dog ran into one of the passages in pursuit of a rat, and the two raced in the direction of Red Abbey. The dog got home safely, but not by the way he had entered, suggesting there was another exit somewhere. It is recorded that at the time of that discovery cartloads of bones were taken out, but no skulls. It was reasoned by the people present at this exhumation that the passageways were the mortuary vaults of the abbey.

ELIZABETH FORT

In the sixteenth century an improved type of fortification was developed to deal with changes in warfare technology. Gunpowder had been in use in Europe since the fourteenth century, but it was only in the mid-1500s that musket guns began to be used. No longer was a large castle the safest place to be. Instead, star-shaped fortresses

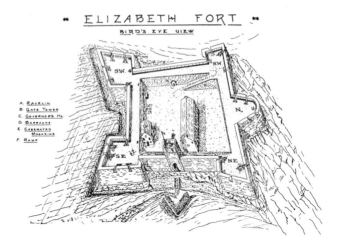

Plan of Elizabeth Fort in 1690.

were deemed the best defence. The distinctive star-shaped plan was developed in Italy in the first three decades of the sixteenth century, based on designs by Giuliano Sangallo, an Italian military engineer. Angle bastions were constructed at the corners of all of the enclosing walls. This enabled the occupying garrison to concentrate its fire-power on any attacking force in a thirty-metre area immediately in front of the fort

In January 1590, Queen Elizabeth I ordered that star-shaped forts be constructed outside the town walls of each major Irish coastal walled town, in particular Waterford, Limerick, Galway and Cork. In Cork, the construction of the new fort was delayed by the ongoing rebellions by the Native Irish. In 1599 a new Lord President of Ireland, Sir George Carew, was appointed to quell the risings. After the Spanish occupation of Kinsale in 1601, Carew decided that Cork –Harbour had to be defended immediately. A star-shaped fort was constructed on Haubowline Island in the harbour, and a second fort was constructed in Kinsale Harbour called James Fort (after James I). In 1601 a star-shaped fort was constructed within the city itself, just outside South Gate Drawbridge on a cliffside that overshadowed and protected the southern road leading into the walled town, now known as Barrack Street. This was called Elizabeth Fort (after Elizabeth I), a name that has remained to the present day.

Built of limestone, timber and earth, the fort was erected on top of a rocky outcrop and early representations show that it was an irregular fortification in design with stone walls on three sides and an earthen bank facing the walled town. The cliff provided protection on one side, whilst around the other three sides a dry moat had been cut into the rock and could be crossed only by a drawbridge. The entrance was further protected by a gate tower and a portcullis. None of the original fort can be seen today.

The fort was garrisoned by October 1602 even though it was unfinished. In 1603, as a result of Cork's refusal to honour the crowning of the Catholic King James I, the fort was attacked by Irish rebels who caused considerable damage to the main structure and stole its arsenal. The Lord Deputy of Cork, Lord Mountjoy, and his forces quickly regained control of the town and forced the unwilling citizens to rebuild the fort. The rebuilding began c.1624 and the old drawbridge was substituted with a causeway, a mound of earth and a more elaborate gateway on the eastern side, most of which was replaced. The repaired structure was called New Fort, but none of it remains today.

In 1649 the ramparts, or defensive walls, were increased to a height of nearly eight metres. By 1690, about 200 English soldiers were employed to man the garrison. Twenty-one cannons were located around the top of the fortification. Each cannon required eight men to operate it – four men to operate the firing mechanism and four men to guard the ammunition.

In the seventeenth century, the English government classified Elizabeth Fort as a virtually impregnable defence work. In 1690, it had five distinct out-shots or bastions. Whilst designed for all-round defence, each of the bastions was capable of acting independently as a 'last-ditch' stronghold. The bastions on the southern side were considerably stronger and larger than those on the northern side, indicating that the designer was well aware of the vulnerabilities of the fort. The foundation of the fortress, which was solid rock, ruled out undermining. An effort was also made to strengthen the entrance area. Here a double wall, double gateway and fifteen-metre-high tower were built. Today, the double walls and entrance can still be seen, but the tower is long gone.

It is unfortunate that much of the documentation describing the layout and rebuilding of the fort from 1719 to the present day has been lost. All that is known is that the encompassing star-shaped bastion remained unchanged. It is also known that in 1719 the fort became a British military barracks and the ramparts had to be thinned to make space for new rooms to accommodate 700 men.

In 1806 a new barracks was constructed to the northeast of the city (now Collins Barracks), and the barracks within Elizabeth Fort became a Female Convict Prison. Samuel Lewis, an Irish historian, related that in 1837 there were 250 inmates, brought from all parts of the country. Many of these women were housed here until ships became available to convey them to other British colonial outposts, in particular New South Wales in Australia.

In the late nineteenth century, Elizabeth Fort was used as a station for the Cork City Artillery Militia. In 1920–21, the fort was occupied by the Royal Irish Constabulary and was handed over to the Irish government. A year later, in 1922, the existing internal buildings of the fort were burned down by Anti-Treaty forces during the Civil War. The walls and bastions of the fort were undamaged. A few years later, a Garda station was set up inside the fort and is still in operation today. Never excavated, Elizabeth Fort no doubt houses a wealth of stories waiting to be discovered.

ST FINBARRE'S CATHEDRAL

St FinBarre's Church of Ireland Cathedral occupies the site of the ancient seventh-century monastery of St FinBarre and is the third church on the site. The first was taken down in 1735 after sustaining massive damage during the Siege of Cork. This small medieval church was reputed to have been the place where poet Edmund Spenser married his second wife, Elizabeth Boyle, in 1594. The second, eighteenth-century church was consecrated in 1735. It was a classical building, which retained the original tower of the first church. It was taken down in 1865 to make way for, in the words of Bishop Gregg, bishop of Cork, 'a structure more worthy of the name, Cork Cathedral'.

In 1863 a competition was launched to find a suitable architect for the new cathedral. The brief stated that the new cathedral should be erected at a cost not exceeding £15,000, that provision should be made for 700 seats, with a chapter house and a vestry, although galleries were not required. The design should be presented under seal, motto, or cipher, that is, a symbol or code. It was further stated that 'designs in the pointed style [Gothic] of architecture are likely to obtain a preference'. Out of sixty-eight entrants from Ireland, Britain and the Continent, the unanimous choice was for the design by William Burges called *Non Mortuus Sed Virescrit*, or 'He is not dead but flourishing'. The basic plan of this design consisted of a central nave, or aisle, with two side aisles in a semicircle, forming an ambulatory around the altar.

On 12 January 1865, the Bishop of Cork laid the first stone of the new cathedral. Once he had secured the contract, Burges began

The Western Portal at St FinBarre's Cathedral is a beautifully wrought doorway made of bronze and silver.

restyling his designs, making them grander and pushing the cost up. The major changes included: another bay added to the choir (£600); barrel vaults to replace wooden ceilings in the aisles; ashlar facing instead of rubble masonry; limestone instead of sandstone for the exterior; Stourton stone instead of Portland stone for the interior crossing-piers, or masonry supports; the western towers were made taller; the number of portal doors was increased from one to three;

and a separate vestry was added, which was eventually constructed in 1896 along with a chapter house that was completed in 1904.

Burges was fortunate that Bishop Gregg had a lifelong interest in fundraising. Indeed, by 1864, two years into the project, £9,000 had been raised to make up the shortfall; Gregg's efforts continued for another twelve years.

During the summer of 1870, crosses were placed in the transepts, the roof was slated and the famous Resurrection (Golden) Angel was added. Floors were flagged, walls plastered and a new organ arrived from London. On 30 November 1870, the cathedral was consecrated, although by that date no more than its shell had been built. Only the lower storeys of the towers were finished, so these were covered with temporary roofs for protection.

There were 1,260 pieces of sculpted stone planned for the cathedral and Burges personally designed each one. Mr Nicholls modelled every one in plaster, except for the figures in the western portals and the four Evangelists around the rose window. Each one was sculpted *in situ* by R McLeod and his staff of local stonemasons. Great care was taken to ensure that every piece was executed to a consistently high standard. This was a process that was to take a decade. Burges, Nicholls and McLeod made a good team. In light of this, Burges was anxious to complete the western façade while all three were alive, claiming that life was short and uncertain. Ironically, Bishop Gregg died within a fortnight and Burges within three years of that statement. Nicholls had not completed the figures of the ten virgins and sixteen saints in the western portals at the time of his death in 1883. They were completed by the team of Chapple and Pullan of John Street, London.

William H Crawford financed the completion of the carving of the western façade, which included the statues in the three portals. The five wise virgins and five foolish virgins are depicted with Christ, with the bridegroom as the central figure. In addition to these, gargoyles of fine workmanship and detail occupy the outside walls. These represent the conflict of good and evil within the soul of a Christian.

Burges assembled the very finest artists and craftsmen to create the stained glass, woodwork, mosaics and metalwork, all under his own guidance. In the case of the stained-glass windows, Burges selected the icons that would appear in the glass and took control of all stages of production, especially the initial sketching, cartooning and manufacture. He selected the theme of Revelation, which complemented the interior sculpture. The images on the glass run in a cycle from The Creation in the western Rose window to the vision of God's throne, from the Book of Apocalypse, in the most easterly window of the ambulatory.

Burges produced cartoons for all but six of the twenty-seven clerestory windows, for a 'wheel' window in the west end and, perhaps, for the round windows in the north transept. The clerestory is the upper part of the central nave, which rises clear of the rest of the building and has its own row of windows. It was argued at the time that the design of the stained-glass windows was among the best of the period.

In the case of the metalwork, the nine wrought iron screens separating chancel and ambulatory were executed by Hart & Co. in 1876–77. The famous David Door – located in the southern section of the cathedral – was executed in 1889, eight years after Burges's death. It was cast in bronze by Hatfield and inlaid with silver by Barkentin and Krall.

The women of Cork presented the lectern. Nicholls was responsible for its modelling, while the design had already been prepared by Burges in 1856 for his tender for the design of Lille Cathedral in France. Inlay and mosaic were important methods in Burges's work. The low choir wall is composed of veined white marble, set with moulded alabaster, red and green marbles and gold mosaics. The altar itself is made of carved oak on black marble inlaid with mosaic. The altar was erected in Bishop Gregg's memory in 1879. The mosaic pavement of the apse was also designed by Burges and was executed by Italian artists from Udine. It is made from marble mined in the Pyrenees Mountains. The theme for the mosaic was taken from St Matthew's pronouncement: 'The kingdom of Heaven is like unto a net that was cast into the sea and gathered of every kind.'

The pulpit was designed in 1873 and finished in 1874, but was not painted until much later by Eileen Dann. The Bishop's Throne is an outstanding piece. It is located in the altar area and consists of approximately fifteen metres of carved oak. On the seat are three wooden panels bearing the carved heads of twenty bishops of the See of Cork, including St FinBarre. Designed by Burges, modelled by Nicholls and executed by Walden, the Throne was exhibited at the Royal Academy in London in 1877 and at the Paris Exhibition in 1878 before being placed in position in the cathedral in 1878. The *sedilia*, a specially designed seat for the President and his assistants at the Eucharist, also came from Walden's workshop in 1879–80.

Above the altar the sanctuary roof is beautifully ornamented. On the left, seven angels are depicted holding seven churches, the last of which is St FinBarre's Cathedral. On the right, seven angels can be seen holding seven golden candlesticks. The ceiling was painted in 1935 by Professor EW Tristram in accordance with Burges's designs. Supporting the ornate roof are large columns of Bath stone, while the walls are red Cork marble.

The organ was built by Messrs Hill and Son, and originally stood in the west gallery. It was transferred to the north transept in 1889 because the pipes obscured the view from the west windows. To accommodate it, the transept was excavated to a depth of over four metres, and in this hollow the organ was placed. The bell tower houses eight bells, all cast by Abel Rudhall of Gloucester in 1751, the same company that manufactured the bells of Shandon.

William Burges died after a short illness on 20 April 1881. A window in the ambulatory of the cathedral is dedicated to his memory. He left behind designs for the completion and decoration of the church. His instructions were faithfully carried out, and the cathedral is as much a paean to his sense of perfection and dedication as it is to the Protestant community who supported its building in every way possible.

UNIVERSITY COLLEGE CORK

The idea of establishing a university at Cork took hold in the early 1800s. At this time, reform in the British university system meant that the professional and commercial middle classes now shared with the upper classes the privilege of third-level education. As a result, the demand for provincial colleges in Britain and in Ireland grew. In the late 1830s, the Munster Provincial College Committee was established to campaign for a university to be built in the city. The Committee was headed by numerous Cork mercantile families, such as the Beamishes, and by Westminster MPs living in County Cork. The most influential of these were Thomas Wyse (Waterford City MP) and William Smith O'Brien (Limerick County MP). Both men shared a desire to see a college built in Munster, but they fell out on numerous occasions as to its location. Wyse wanted it to be in Cork, while O'Brien wanted it to be in Limerick. As a result, rival committees were set up who campaigned separately. In the end, Cork's application was approved.

In 1845 the Colleges of Ireland Act was passed, which provided funding to establish one or more colleges in Ireland. It was initially decided to establish Queen's Colleges (after Queen Victoria) in Belfast and Cork, followed later by a third institution in Galway.

A site to the west of the city on a flat limestone outcrop was chosen for the new building. Private architects were chosen to draw up the designs. Sir Thomas Deane was the most obvious choice for a major government commission as he was the most experienced. The requirements of the college were laid down clearly from the start, for example, no residential provision was necessary for the students or professors, except for the president and vice-president.

There was, however, no stipulation regarding the architectural style. Deane chose to adopt the Tudor Domestic Gothic style. He planned it as a quadrangle, with three sides enclosed. It is likely that he looked to Oxford College for inspiration, especially to the designs of William Henry Hill who was originally from Cork. Similarities with the tower and cloister design of Magdalen College, Oxford, are

The Ogham stone corridor in the north wing of the Quadrangle at UCC, which houses approximately thirty stones.

apparent. Cork's Aula Maxima, or Great Hall, located in the north wing, was probably inspired by the recently opened hall and library at Lincoln's Inn College in London, while the Gothic-style windows resemble those designed by Francis Johnston for the Chapel Royal at Dublin Castle.

One of the first problems Deane encountered was the question of where to place the entrances to the college. He was reluctant to accept the proposal that one of the main entrances should be adjacent to the County Jail as he did not wish to have lecturers crossing the paths of 'dishonourable' people. Eventually he succumbed to the will of the Committee and included the entrance. The second entrance was a pedestrian footbridge from the Western Road. This bridge was swept away in a flood in 1916 and was replaced with a new bridge in 1928, which is still in use.

The building work began in early 1847 and was completed within two years. The Committee was anxious to finish the college for the visit of Queen Victoria to the site on 3 August 1849. The Royal visit was marked by the unveiling of a statue of the queen, which is located on the roof of the Aula Maxima, on the east-facing gable.

Professors were appointed on 4 August 1849, and on 30 October 1849 the college welcomed its first students. The first name on the registration book was Denis Bullen, aged fifteen, whose father was Professor of Surgery at the college. In all, 115 students enrolled in the faculties of medicine, arts and law. In the period from 1852 to 1859, forty-nine Bachelor of Arts degrees were conferred. The first admission of female students to Queen's College Cork did not take place until October 1885. In 1910, Mary Ryan simultaneously became Professor of Romance Languages and the first female professor in Ireland.

One of the college's most eminent professors was mathematician George Boole. A native of Lincoln in England, he began his career as an assistant at a school in Lincoln and shortly after established his own successful educational establishment in the area. In 1844, Boole was awarded a gold medal by the Royal Society and developed a new branch of mathematics known as Boolean Algebra, which led eventually to the development of computer science. He began to submit papers to the Cambridge and Dublin Mathematical Journals and shortly afterward published *The Mathematical Analysis of Logic*. Even though he did not hold a primary university degree, Boole was nonetheless appointed Professor of Mathematics at Cork in 1854. Just ten years later, in December 1864, Boole died from pneumonia after walking four miles to the college from Ballintemple in a rainstorm. Boole is still remembered in UCC today, especially in the Aula Maxima where a large stained-glass window depicts the great mathematician seated at his writing desk, watched over by Aristotle and Euclid. He is also invoked in the name of the college's central library, Boole Library.

One of the most notable additions to the Quadrangle was the famous Ogham stone collection, numbering thirty in all and representing the largest collection of Ogham stones on display in Ireland. The stones are ancient gravestones, each one marking the burial place of a distinguished person in a Celtic tribe. They date from the Early Christian era and are unique in that they bear one of the earliest forms of writing. Letters, represented by groups of grooves and notches etched onto the stone, record simple genealogical statements.

One of the more controversial stones added to the Ogham collection came from a ringfort at Knockshanawee in County Cork. Archaeologist RAS Macalister, then president of the college (1904–19), and the first Professor of Archaeology Bertram Windele decided to transfer Ogham stones from the chamber of the ringfort to UCC. In addition, two decorated cup-and-circle stones, a rotary quern stone for grinding corn and a cross-inscribed slab were also marked down for the college's collection. Local antiquaries opposed the move because the stones in question were supporting the roof of the chamber, which would collapse if the stones were dislodged. Other critics condemned the plan as 'scientific vandalism'. Macalister and Windele ignored all detractors and took the items. They can still be seen in UCC today.

Under the Irish Universities Act 1908, two new universities – the National University of Ireland and Queen's University Belfast – were established, and on 31 October 1909 the term 'Royal University' was dissolved. By virtue of the Universities Act 1997, UCC became known as the National University of Ireland, Cork. The governing body has since extended the legal name of the university to University College Cork, National University of Ireland, Cork.

Located on the grounds of UCC, Honan Chapel is regarded as an outstanding example of Irish ecclesiastical architecture. The chapel,

James F McMullen's exquisite and well-proportioned
Honan Chapel can be seen on the grounds of UCC.

constructed in 1915 and designed by James F McMullen, is a modern
reconstruction in the Hiberno-Romanesque style, which is derived
from tenth-century church buildings, such as Cormac's Chapel at
Cashel, County Tipperary. The church is dedicated to St FinBarre
and was built through the generosity of the Honan family. Apart from
its architecture, the chapel is noted for the quality of its nineteen
stained-glass windows, eleven of which were designed and made by
Harry Clarke, whilst the remaining eight were designed by a number
of artists from the studio of Sarah Purser. Also of interest is the
mosaic floor depicting the signs of the zodiac, the river of life and
various animals of the earth and the heavens. As part of the Honan
bequest, an elaborate biology institute was established in a building
next to the Chapel. In 2002 the institute's building was demolished
to make way for a larger student centre and to provide more recrea-
tional space.

   The Crawford Observatory was constructed and fitted out in 1879
through the generosity of William Crawford and the Duke of Devonshire. The building reflects the ecclesiastical style of the early buildings at UCC and is one of very few in Britain and Ireland with Gothic
features. The general plan follows the layout originally developed in
eighteenth-century Scandinavian observatories, with a two-storey
central section flanked by single-storey wings, one to the east and

one to the west. The observatory incorporates an equatorially mounted telescope by Howard Grubb of Dublin, which received a gold medal at the Paris Exhibition in 1879 prior to its installation at UCC. It houses a siderosatic telescope, a transit circle of novel construction and original clock arrangements. The telescope has not been used in recent decades, but UCC aims to restore the observatory to good working order.

Today, University College Cork has 12,000 students and 1,700 staff and is the lifeblood of the city. The improvement and expansion of the campus is ongoing. Recently a new student centre, Áras na Mac Léinn, opened and boasts an impressive glass frontage. In 2003 a new art gallery and restaurant got underway, and a new commerce building called the O'Rahilly Building (Alfred O'Rahilly, president of UCC 1945–54) has been carefully designed to complement the architecture of the original white limestone Quadrangle.

CALLANAN'S TOWER

Amidst all the construction in the nineteenth century, one particularly interesting venture was opened off Barrack Street and Tower Street in 1865. It was a large tower and formal gardens owned and created by Michael Callanan, a city merchant. Callanan's vision was inspired by the Crystal Palace Exhibition in London, which he had visited in 1851. Here, an English arboretical architect, Sir Joseph Paxton, had designed a stylised glass building to house the Hyde Park Exhibition. Three years later, in 1854, the structure was removed, extensively enlarged and set up permanently in Sydenham, just outside London. Exhibitions, concerts,

Callanan's Tower projecting from the south side of the city.

conferences and sporting events were held at the Crystal Palace until it was destroyed by fire in 1936.

Callanan decided to build a similar complex on a smaller scale. Instead of Paxton's glass complex, a tall limestone tower would provide the focal point. Ornamental gardens were planned and a tower approximately twenty-five to thirty metres tall was built in imitation of a medieval castle, with over 100 steps and crenellations. From the top, one could enjoy a panoramic view of the city. For those who wished to avail of the gardens there was a fee, but we do not know the sum charged. An 1871 advertisement reminded citizens that the tower had been erected for the sole benefit of the poor of the city. Accordingly, relief boxes for the Protestant and Roman Catholic parishes were placed at the entrance to the tower, and could be opened only by officers of the respective communities.

The estimated cost of the scheme was £50,000. Once the gardens and tower were in place, Callanan attempted to recoup some of his initial outlay by attracting investment. Accordingly, he placed advertisements in local street directories and newspapers. An account in a local directory in 1871 praised the tower gardens highly:

> 'The attractions of the Tower Gardens are selected so as to afford a variety which will combine with advantages derivable from nature and art. From the summit of the tower, which is built on one of the most elevated positions about Cork, the visitor can enjoy a bird's eye view of the entire city and suburbs.'

The surrounding 'pleasure grounds' comprised an area of seven acres. Walks extended upwards for about a mile. Callanan detailed that here 'pure bracing air' could be enjoyed in a countryside-like environment, the advantage being that this amenity was just minutes' walk from the city. Callanan mentioned that a new and spacious concert hall was due to be built and would open in July 1872; it was never built. Rustic seats, summer-houses, grottoes and fountains were dotted about the grounds.

The grounds had facilities for athletics, gymnastics and Olympic games. Archery and cricket grounds were provided, along with a trapeze, dumb-bells and all the appliances of an open-air gymnasium. Callanan remarked that he gained much pleasure in directing the attention of 'amateurs and gentlemen to the facilities which the establishment offers for the practice of such games as Cricket, Lawn

Billiards, Croquet, American and English Bowls, Quoits, and all the newest and most fashionable sports.' A proposed racket court and ball alley were never constructed. An extensive racecourse was laid down in lawn grass and afforded a level run of nearly half-a-mile.

Refreshments were also supplied in the gardens. Porter from the old and celebrated firm of Beamish and Crawford, wines, ales and spirits of the best quality could be purchased. Tea, coffee and fruits were supplied during the season. According to Callanan, for the benefit of his patrons care was given to the first principles of order and decorum, and to this end he reserved the right to refuse admission to disorderly or objectionable persons.

By the time *Guy's Street Directory of Cork* was published in 1875–76, the tower gardens were no more. Local tradition has it that the place attracted too many undesirables and that foreign sailors visiting the port treated the gardens as an open-air public house. As a result, it was closed down and Callanan's vision was destroyed. Most of the facilities and buildings were taken down, apart from the viewing tower. Today, the tower is still a prominent landmark on the south side of the city and forms a backdrop to the gardens behind the Tower Bar on Tower Street. It is now the property of the Tower Bar, which owns the tower and is the route of access to it.

FRANCISCAN ABBEY, NORTH MALL

In the twelfth and thirteenth centuries, a number of religious houses were established in the suburbs of the walled town of Cork. On the northern hillside, large tracts of land were owned by the Franciscans who established an abbey on what is now the North Mall. The abbey was founded in 1229 by Dermot McCarthy, King of Desmond, who was loyal to King Henry II. It became commonly known as the North Abbey and flourished for nearly three centuries. Early Franciscan records show that provincial chapters or national gatherings of the Franciscan monks took place at the abbey in 1244 (the first ever chapter held in Ireland), 1288, 1291, 1521 and 1533.

Depictions of the walled town, in particular in the *Pacata Hibernia*, show the North Abbey was built against a rock face. It had at least a church and a belfry, which separated the altar area from the congregation area. In April 1540, a Royal survey detailed that the

abbey comprised one hall, one kitchen, one cloister, six large dormitory chambers for the monks, six cellars, a watermill, a fishing place
for salmon, a salmon weir and several plots of land in the townland of
Teampall na mBrathair, or Church of the Monks. The abbey also had
a dole house – a dwelling dedicated to helping the impoverished. This
stood just to the east of the main complex, on what is now the site of
North Abbey Square on the North Mall. Placename evidence also suggests that the friars possessed a chapel in the northern hills overlooking the walled town known as Cilleen na Gurranaigh, or The Little
Church of the Groves. In time, this placename changed to Gurradh
na mBráthair, or Friars' Grove, now known as Gurranabrahar.

The old well of the Franciscan Abbey, the waters of
which were once thought
to have curative properties.

Following the survey, the lands of the
abbey were confiscated and it was ordered
that the church and belfry be demolished
and the rest of the buildings be used for
non-religious purposes. The abbey was let
out to a merchant, David Sheghan. By 1562,
the land belonged to John Brown and
Edmond Gould, who were forced to hand it
back to the Catholic Church during Queen
Mary's reign. However, Queen Mary's sister,
Elizabeth I, suppressed the monasteries
again and the lands were passed to a
wealthy merchant named Andrew Skiddy. It
is not known if Skiddy took up residence in
the Abbey complex, but by 1626 most of the
buildings had been demolished, with only
the walls of the church left standing.

Due to political circumstances in Britain, it was only in the mid- to late 1600s
that a Franciscan chapel and house were
built on the site. These buildings still
existed in the early half of the 1700s, but
were destroyed to make way for eighteenth-
and nineteenth-century housing. In 1688, on a Royal visit to Cork,
King James II stayed in the house of the North Abbey.

Perhaps, the best-known feature of the abbey is its water well. The
well is situated at the foot of a rock face, on the grounds of a new bar
called the Abbey Tavern, and is housed within a stone-built well

house. The entrance has a wooden panel with '1688' recorded in iron numbers on it. Although reputed to be a holy well, it is not dedicated to any particular saint. Nonetheless, the water is said to cure sore eyes, consumption and other ailments. Next to the well is a second stone-walled room, which is partially cut out of the rock face. The purpose of this room is unknown. Legend has it that beyond the end wall of the room is an underground passage leading up into the environs of Gurranabraher.

In *History of Cork* (1844), John Windele reported that during digging for the foundations of the current red-brick houses in 1804, a number of stone coffins belonging to the Franciscan abbey were recovered. Amongst these was a stone coffin with a sceptre inscribed on it and an incomplete sentence on the lid in Norman French, reading *Sa Alme hait merci*, which means 'his generosity dislikes thanks'. The location of these stone coffins today is unknown.

Robert Day, another eminent antiquary, related that during digging for the foundations of Herbert's Square on the North Mall in 1896, a stone was discovered with the date '1567' etched on it. In addition, a small plate of metal was found on which was etched a representation of the Nativity and a long description in Dutch. A font and a silver chalice were also discovered, which at the time were recorded as being objects from the chapel that had existed on the site in the early half of the 1600s. Both the font and chalice were sent to White Church Chapel, located just to the north of Cork City, where they can still be seen today.

Two other architectural stone pieces from the North Abbey exist. The first was presented to a Rev. Brother Leonard, a Christian Brother, and was built into the garden wall of his monastery at Peacock Lane in Sunday's Well. Its subsequent history is shrouded in mystery and it has never been recovered. John Dalton, a city historian, drew a sketch of it in 1894 and described it as a broken fragment of a larger piece. The 'G' of the word Gloria was broken off; the letters I.M. represented the initials of Jesus and Mary. The date on the stone was 1590.

The second stone was a cut-stone head from one of the abbey's windows. In architectural terms, it was a double ogee-headed piece. The letters S.B.M.C. stand out. Dalton believed that these letters stood for *Sancta Beata Mater Christi,* or Blessed Virgin Mother of Christ. This stone can still be seen today in the distillery wall of

Wise's Distillery (established 1779) at the foot of Wise's Hill. It is said to mark the spot of another holy well named Tobar na Bhrianach, which means 'the well of learning, or eloquence'. This well, now long gone, is mentioned in a Franciscan deed in 1588 as being in the possession of the abbey. It is reputed that people used to come from around the country in the early 1700s to take water from the well, however on one or two occasions the excise authorities caught some persons bringing out buckets of a different kind of *uisce* – *uisce beatha,* or whiskey, instead of water, which they had taken from the adjacent distillery. The owners, the Wise family, were forced to stop

North Mall, once the site of the North Abbey,
dedicated to Our Lady.

the practice of allowing visitors to the well and it was closed. The stone from the Abbey was placed on the site to mark its location.

Apart from the well and associated rooms, several of the garden walls behind the buildings that front the North Mall possess architectural features from the medieval abbey. In some, stone corbels can be seen jutting out from the wall. These would have been used to support timber roof beams. The same design can be seen in the more complete Franciscan Abbey at Kilcrea in the Lee Valley, County Cork.

Between 1730 and 1750, the Franciscan order moved from the North Mall to three separate areas in the city. The first site was adjacent to Shandon, the second in Cotner's Lane in the city centre, between North Main Street and the Coal Market, and the third location was near the area of Oliver Plunkett Street, where it meets the

Grand Parade. By 1750, the Franciscans had moved again and had established a central friary in Broad Lane, which today is part of the site of St Francis Church on Liberty Street. In 1771, the friars made another move, this time to the opposite side of Little Cross Street (again part of the present site of St Francis Church). It is here that the Franciscan order has remained.

CORK CITY JAIL

In the medieval period, the central prison in Cork was located at North Gate Drawbridge, while the county jail was located at South Gate Drawbridge. In 1712–13, the drawbridge towers were replaced by three-storey jails, which continued in operation until the late 1700s. In the late 1700s, city officials and a group of prison inspectors proposed that, due to appalling conditions and overcrowding, both jaiols be refurbished. In early 1824, city officials first mooted the idea of a new jail located away from the commercial heart of the city, in the western suburbs. Subsequently, a new Cork County Jail was constructed in 1791, designed by Michael Shanahan who also designed the eighteenth-century St Patrick's Bridge. In 1808 it was proposed that a new city jail be constructed as well, outside the former medieval centre.

The front entrance to the former Cork City Jail.
Owen Ryan was hanged right in front of the doorway,
now the entrance to an elaborate heritage centre.

The first site chosen for the new city jail was located west of the North Mall in an area known as O'Reilly's Marsh and the Sally Gardens, now close to the site of Wise's Distillery. However, due to the risk of flooding, a decision was taken to locate the building approximately 1,000 metres to the north, on the hillside at Sunday's Well. A grant of £20,000 was given by the English Parliament to finance its construction. Sir Thomas Deane was appointed architect, Mr Richard Natter from Carrigdubh was appointed builder. Building commenced in 1821, using locally quarried sandstone. About 150 cells were built in the three-storey complex, which was enclosed by a high, solid wall. On 17 August 1824 the first prisoners arrived at the jail.

An account in a street directory by Pigot & Co. in 1824 described the magnificent views from Sunday's Well, but also described the presence of the new jail, which it compared to a castle. In addition, it recorded that at each side of the entrance tower was a crenellated stone tower, and over the main door was a spot where male criminals were executed by hanging. In April 1828 the first public execution took place outside the main gate. Mr Owen Ryan, a Corkman of unknown occupation, was hanged for the crime of rape. Bells tolled and black flags fluttered in the wind on top of the jail as Ryan met his demise, witnessed by the high sheriff and the governor of the jail. Public executions took place here until 1868.

By 1836, on average 1,600 prisoners, mainly women, were incarcerated in the jail each year. The prison was divided into a number of sections. The wing west of the governor's quarters housed male prisoners, while female prisoners were housed in the east wing. The smaller areas on either side of the governor's quarters were occupied by staff rooms and prison offices. A small block on the eastern side housed the solitary confinement cells. Most prisoners had short stays as their crimes were not serious, hooliganism, larceny, drunkenness and disorderly behaviour being the main offences. Hard labour was the usual punishment handed down to adult offenders and ranged from stone-breaking and moving tread wheels to sewing and manufacturing mats and other fabrics. Indeed, prior to 1858, when the jail was connected to the city reservoirs, a tread wheel was used to raise water. This wheel was operated on a five-hour daily shift by hard labour prisoners.

The remaining numbers were made up of debtors and those involved in Nationalist or 'anti-Crown' activities. The debtors' prison was divided into two parts: pauper debtors and gentlemen debtors. In 1848–49, members of the Young Ireland group – James Mountaine, Denny Lane, Terence Bellew McManus and Ralph and Isaac Varian – were incarcerated in the prison. During the Fenian risings of 1865, Cork Fenians Brian Dillon and John Sarsfield Casey were also imprisoned here for a short time.

In summertime, cell doors were unlocked at 6am and relocked at 6pm. This freedom period was reduced by two hours in winter. Due to the severe winters, in 1858 the clothes of male and female prisoners were changed from coarse flax to wool. In addition, hot air was piped into a number of cells. Breakfast consisted of Indian meal, rice and a pint of milk, while dinner was brown bread and two pints of milk; females received a smaller ration than males. Schooling was given to convicted children who could be admitted as young as ten. The punishment for juveniles for common crimes, such as larceny, was usually a number of lashes with the whip.

An interesting account of life in the prison was given by an unknown occupant of the jail in the 1850s: 'The cells where we slept were narrow and ill-ventilated, connected by a common corridor, which opened on to a room larger than one of the sleeping cells. This room we used as a parlour. It was cut off from the rest of the prison by heavy doors with locks, bars and bolts.'

In 1868 the debtors' prison closed and the last of the public executions took place. In 1878 the jail became an all-women's prison and the male prisoners were sent to the County Jail on Western Road. The high number of female convicts reflects the fact that many women from the poorer classes turned to crime to support their families.

During a period of civil unrest in the 1920s, the jail was used to imprison members of the IRA. Famous political internees included Constance Markievicz and Frank O'Connor. Many members of Cumann na mBan also spent time in the cells, especially one patriotic Corkwoman, Mary Bowles. In October 1923, political prisoners in Mountjoy Jail, Dublin, embarked on a hunger strike, and soon anti-Treaty prisoners all over Ireland had joined them. In Cork, nearly 100 prisoners went on hunger strike. In response, Cork Corporation allowed the unconditional release of most of them, to safeguard their health. The scribblings and drawings made by the imprisoned men and women are still preserved on the cell walls.

In 1927 the jail became the Cork Broadcast Station and subsequently all jail fittings were sold off. The radio station closed in 1958 and the building was taken over by the Department of Posts and Telegraphs as a training school. In the 1970s and early 1980s the jail was used as a store for poles and drums, a practice that was eventually phased out in the 1980s. In 1992 plans were drawn up to open the jail as a heritage centre. Much of the building has been remarkably restored and it is now one of Cork's premier heritage sites. In recent times a radio museum has also been added to celebrate the Cork Broadcast Station.

ST ANNE'S CHURCH, SHANDON

St Anne's Church was built in 1722 to replace the older church of St Mary's, Shandon, which was destroyed in the Siege of Cork. It is situated a short distance from St Patrick's Street, its giant 'pepper canister' steeple a familiar sight on the north side of the city. Shandon comes from the Irish *sean dún*, which means 'old fort' and refers to the ringfort of the MacCarthaigh clan who once lived in the area. The site of the fort is now occupied by the Firkin Crane Dance Centre.

The architectural style of the church and tower is early English. A peculiar feature of the tall tower, standing approximately forty metres high, is that the north and east sides are red sandstone, while the south and west sides are grey hewn limestone. The limestone came from the ruins of the Franciscan Abbey, while the sandstone came from Shandon Castle. Rising from the main tower, which is in the shape of a telescope, are three further tiers ending in a curved dome. Above this is a gilt ball, which is crowned by the cardinal

One face of the 'Four-faced Liar' that graces St Anne's Church, Shandon.

points – north, south, west and east – and a weather vane in the form of a giant fish, commonly known in Cork as 'the Goldy Fish'. This impressive weather vane, almost five metres long, represents an important Cork industry, salmon fishing, as well as symbolising the name of Jesus.

In 1750 the famous bells of Shandon were cast by the firm of Abel Rudhall in Gloucester, but it was another two years before they were installed in the tower. The bells were first heard on 7 December 1752, to announce the marriage of a Mr Henry Harding to Miss Catherine Dorman. Each of the eight bells has its own inscription, as follows: (1) when us you ring we'll sweetly sing; (2) God preserve the Church and King; (3) health and prosperity to all our benefactors; (4) peace and good neighbourhood; (5) prosperity to the city; (6) we were all cast at Gloucester in England by Abel Rudhall 1750; (7) since generosity has opened our mouths, our tongues shall sing aloud its praise; and (8) I to the Church, the living call and to the grave do summon all. Four of the bells have been recast since their first use, one in 1869 and the others in 1908. Fortunately, all of the bells still have their original inscriptions and are still *in situ* in the belfry.

The famous clock of Shandon with its four white faces was installed by Cork Corporation in 1847 and was made by James Mangan, a local watch- and clockmaker. He made several other notable clocks throughout Munster, including the ornate clock on St Patrick's Street, outside the entrance to Merchant's Quay Shopping Centre. The clock on Shandon is an efficient time-keeper except for the fact that the minute hands on the east and west faces always run ahead of their accomplices on the north and south faces in the ascent from the half-hour to the hour, which is why it is known as 'the Four-faced Liar'. Complete concurrence is achieved once more on the hour. The machinery of the clock is said to weigh two tonnes, with each dial measuring four metres in diameter. An inscription on the machinery warns ominously: *Passenger measure your time, for time is the measure of your being.*

It is very much worth the ascent of over 100 steps up to the clock machinery section and on to the bell tower. As well as being able to examine the mechanics of the Four-faced Liar, the visitor can also avail of the opportunity to play famous tunes on the bells. Emerging onto the parapet outside the bell tower, one is met with a breath-taking view across the city.

For nearly 250 years, the bells of St Anne's, Shandon, have been ringing throughout Cork City. Their fame has spread all over the world, especially with the famous words of Rev. Francis Mahony's (or Fr Prout) poem 'The Bells of Shandon' echoing behind their history.

> With deep affection and recollection,
> I often think of those Shandon Bells,
> whose sounds so wild would, in days of childhood,
> fling round my cradle their spells.

The priest-poet's remains lie in a family vault close to the foot of the steeple, where the pealing of the bells can reverberate through eternity.

BUTTER MARKET

By the mid-1700s, the butter industry in Cork had grown to such an extent that a decision was taken to establish an institution to control and develop its potential. Consequently, in 1769 the Committee of Butter Merchants began their work. Locating themselves in a simple purpose-built building adjacent to Shandon, the group comprised twenty-one members chosen by the city's merchants. The first ten were known as senior members and would serve a year in office. The second ten were junior members and would serve two years in office, becoming senior members in their second year. The remaining member was the treasurer, a post filled by annual election. The committee was a voluntary institution and had no legal status. Unfortunately, as with so much of Cork's history, there is no comprehensive record for the development of the butter market. However, there are minute manuscripts for the Cork Committee of Butter Merchants and the *Reports of the Select Committee on the Butter Trade of Ireland*.

In May 1770 the Committee ordered that all butter to be exported from Cork was to be examined by appointed inspectors. Firstly, they would examine and determine the quality and weight of the butter. Secondly, they would examine and report on the manner of packing, checking for any signs of fraudulent practices. The inspectors were well paid and received a pension. However, they were limited to a

three-month term of office. In addition, a severe penalty was imposed
on the inspector if he made a poor judgement, or was found to be in
conspiracy with a merchant.

Farmers either brought their butter to market, or hired a broker
to bring it from the country to the town. It did not matter at what
time the farmer or broker arrived as the market was open night and
day to facilitate the huge volume of trade. All butter transacted in
the Butter Market had to be placed in wooden casks called firkins. In
light of this, Inspectors of Empty Casks were appointed. They were
responsible for inspecting each cask before handing it over to the

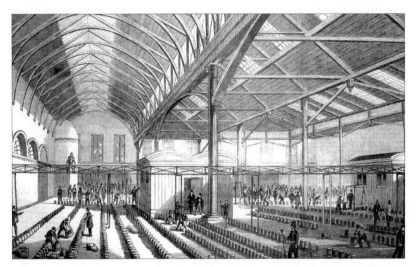

A busy scene of inspectors examining firkins of butter in the Cork Butter Market,
as depicted by the *Illustrated London News* on 2 April 1859.

farmer to be filled with butter. When the full firkins were returned to
the weigh-house by the farmer, the inspectors examined them again
to ensure proper practice. The wooden casks were subject to specific
restrictions. The cask had to be made from seasoned oak, sycamore,
or beech. Oak was particularly suitable for preserving butter on
long-distance voyages. All firkins being shipped to far-flung destina-
tions, such as Brazil and the West Indies, had to be bound in iron
hoops. A small portion of butter was taken out to allow for pickle to
be added, which further preserved the taste.

The Committee went to great lengths to prevent any sort of profi-
teering or collusion. A porter received the firkin of butter, initialised
it, chalked each cask and arranged them in lots for inspection the

following day. The number of lots depended on the number of inspectors available. In the morning, the inspectors drew a lot number. No inspector knew until the last moment which casks he would be inspecting. The inspectors examined each cask and then awarded the butter a 'first', 'second', 'third', 'fourth', 'fifth', or 'sixth'. First was 'superfine' (excellent quality), while Sixth butter was 'grease' (very poor quality). Cork Firsts were nearly always sent to Lisbon, while Cork Seconds were sent to the West Indies. Cork Thirds were sent to Southern England and to certain Scottish ports.

Once the butter had been checked, the quality was noted and recorded along with the name of the supplier. Appeals could be lodged regarding the quality mark allocated to any cask. The cask was taken to the weigh-house, also located within the building, to be checked by the weigh-master. Here it was branded with its mark and weight. The word 'Cork' was included on all casks, for example, 'Cork Firsts', 'Cork Seconds', etc. This classification system was strictly enforced and anyone found to be in breach of the regulations was punished. The local newspapers were given the names and deeds of misdoers to print for all to see. In some cases, prison sentences could also be expected. The most common offence was tampering with quality marks, or 'do-it-yourself' branding. To combat this, slight variations in the type of branding used were introduced regularly.

By the mid-1800s, the butter market had grown to such an extent that it was necessary to expand the premises. In 1849 an elaborate Roman temple-style portico, designed by Sir John Benson, was added to the front of the building. Just a decade or two later, in the late 1800s, there was a distinct decline in the economic fortunes of the city and the once-booming profits of the export trade in agricultural produce declined. In 1858, 428,000 firkins of butter were being exported per annum, by 1891 this was down to 170,000 firkins. Competitive European prices undercut the prices set by the butter market at Cork. In addition, the city's best consumer, the British citizen, favoured neater packaging, smaller and more exact weights, improved colour, texture and taste; qualities that Cork butter did not possess. The quantity of butter exported decreased steadily until eventually the Cork Butter Market closed in 1924. Today, part of the Butter Market is a craft centre, whilst smaller areas of it have been enclosed as private gardens. In recent years, a butter museum opened up next to the craft centre in the Tony O'Reilly Centre. Here, everything from old documents to branding irons can be seen.

The market itself may have closed, but one of its pet projects lives on in the form of the Butter Exchange Band. Better known as 'The Buttera', it is one the best-known brass-and-reed bands in the city. Sponsored by the Butter Market, the band was established in 1878 but has antecedents in a confraternity band established by Fr John McNamara, a curate of the North Cathedral. At the time, the band was one of a number in the city but was regarded as more prestigious because of its association with the Butter Market. The biggest event for the band in the twentieth century was the annual Corpus Christi Procession, as well as Christmas and Easter Mass in the cathedral. The band also performed for President John F Kennedy during his visit to Cork in June 1963. One hundred and twenty-five years on, The Buttera remains a much-loved element of city events, still performing as their long tradition dictates.

NORTH CATHEDRAL

The Cathedral of SS. Mary and Anne's, located on the intersection of Griffin Street, Roman Street and Shandon Street, casts a long shadow across Blackpool and Gurranabraher. The present cathedral building was built in the 1860s and is the fifth church on the site since the early 1600s. The first church was built around 1624, but was only dedicated as a parish church in 1635. It is thought that it was located in Coppinger's Lane (now St Rita's Place) and was called the Baptismal Church. Church documents record that the building was evacuated in 1649 due to Cromwell's Age of Commonwealth, which lasted from 1649 to c.1660. During this time the residents of the parish were forced to celebrate Mass in their own houses, in secret and in defiance. The second church was built c.1700 under the direction of Bishop Donough McCarthy, later Bishop of Cork and Cloyne. This new church was constructed in present-day Old Chapel Lane and afterwards was converted into a school, now long gone. The name of the school is not recorded. In 1730 the third church was built on the site of the present cathedral, under the patronage of the Bishop of Cork, Teige McCarthy Rabach.

The nineteenth-century Great Western Door of the North Cathedral, which started out in the seventeenth-century as a simple stone-built Masshouse.

On 4 June 1787 a new bishop of Cork and Cloyne, Francis Moylan, was appointed. His ambition was to build a cathedral for his diocese. Construction began in 1799 and the cathedral was completed nine years later. On Monday, 22 August 1808 the new North Cathedral was dedicated to the Blessed Virgin Mary and St Anne. The church was one of the first ecclesiastical buildings in Cork to be built following the era of the Penal Laws. In addition, it was one of the earliest examples of the neo-Gothic style in the city.

In 1820 a fire swept through the cathedral, leaving a charred skeletal framework and little else. Bishop John Murphy engaged George Richard Pain to oversee the rebuilding. Around 1828 the renovation began, retaining the neo-Gothic style. The side aisles were substituted with a large gallery at the western end, which is still used by the choir today. The main altar was redesigned by John Hogan, with twenty-seven statues of saints placed at intervals around it. The pulpit and *cathedra*, or Bishop's seat, were made of carved oak with beautifully sculpted angels hovering delicately over both.

Between 1862 and 1867 a tower on the western end was added, but the project, overseen by Canon Foley, was hampered by lack of funds. To economise, the facing stones were cut in such a way that they would cover more space. However, when a certain height was reached, the stones with an upright grain shattered and work was halted. On top of this, on 5 July 1869 an article in the *Cork Examiner* declared that the building was an 'edifice worthy only – in external appearance at least – of a country parish'. On the basis of this report, Sir John Benson was approached to redesign the church again.

In 1868, at a meeting of Catholic citizens convened by Bishop Delany, certain alterations and improvements to the church were debated. The aim was to build 'an edifice in whose magnitude and splendour the present unpretending structure will have been completely absorbed as scarcely to be traceable'. Sir John Benson's plans were adopted. His design included a geometrical plan that reflected medieval cathedral architecture. The church would be enlarged to double its size and a nave, choir, chancel with four chapels and transepts with side aisles would be added in the east end. A clerestory would be built over the existing altar to increase the sense of height. The clerestory windows would comprise Galway black and green marble and red Cork marble. The ceilings would be richly ornate. The pillars dividing the main nave from the aisle would be made of Portland stone with red marble ends, and the pillars separating the chancel from the side chapels would be made of Cork red marble with black marble ends. It was intended that the whole of the east end, including the side chapel and choir, be vaulted in masonry. Numerous windows would illuminate the building and stained glass would be added in later years. The internal walls would be lined and dressed with Bath stone and marble. The effect of the interior design, according to Benson, would be awe-inspiring, 'partaking of all the characteristics of breadth and loftiness, massiveness and beauty of construction ... belonging to a grand cathedral.'

Externally, buttresses and parapets surmounted with minarets would be added to the side walls. The existing porch would be substituted with a larger and more elegant one that would project beyond the line of railings, which were to be removed. The eastern end of the church would be square, with a large five-light window of great beauty. The dressings of the windows at the eastern end, the buttresses, cornices, parapets, minarets and the external facing of the wall would be composed principally of finely dressed white limestone, the rest would be made of red sandstone. Due to the incline on which it was built, the eastern end of the building would be 100 feet higher than previously planned. The southern transept would house one of the principal doors, which would be deeply recessed and lined on each side with marble shafts. Over the door, a large rose window would be placed. In the angles formed by the transepts and the chancel extensive sacristies would be built. To complete the cathedral, a spire would be added to the western tower.

The building work commenced straight away and by July 1869 most of the outer features had been completed, including the parapets, spire and minarets. Unfortunately, at this point the project ran into serious financial difficulty and the remaining features were never added. Instead of the proposed spire, four pinnacles gave the tower a distinctive appearance. At a height of forty-six metres, the cathedral stands three metres higher than the tower of Shandon, although Shandon enjoys a better view of the city due to its location.

The bells of the church, cast in the Murphy Foundry, Dublin, were placed in position in 1870. In 1877 Cork Corporation granted extra ground space to the western front of the cathedral to allow for a more dignified approach from Clarence Street (now Gerald Griffin Street) and Shandon Street. At the same time a lane known as Rogerson's Lane was widened, creating further space on the southern side. From then on, the main entrance to the cathedral was from the west.

Just after his death, Benson's proposal for an ornate western door was carried out. Known as the Great Western Door, it borrowed from fourteenth-century design principles, with a pointed arch at the top. The archway is bordered on each side by a scroll-bearing angel and under the apex of the pointed arch, on the tympanum, is the emblem of the Blessed Trinity. Just under the tympanum is a medallion bearing the Diocesan emblem. As Benson's rose window never materialised, lancet windows, or tall pointed windows, were added to create an imposing tracery window to highlight the magnificence of the doorway. These windows were only put into place during renovations in the 1960s.

Another interesting feature of the present cathedral is the crypt. This was primarily used for burials between 1810 and 1876. After the latter date, burials were discontinued. The names of those interred in the crypt are commemorated on a slab that is located outside the mortuary on the northern transept. The Very Rev. Daniel Canon Foley was one of those interred in the crypt. His epitaph reads: 'Through whose untiring exertions this cathedral was enlarged and the tower built (1875).' During renovations in the 1960s, the bones of those buried in the crypt were exhumed and reinterred in St Fin-Barre's Cemetery.

In 1964 the cathedral was extended in length again, resulting in the reconstruction of everything east of the original communion rail. Various new rooms were added, such as a new sacristy, a conference room, a mortuary chapel and a complex of rooms for parish groups. A number of other new features were added: recessional confessionals, heating system, mahogany seating and stations of the cross. The main gallery over the Great Western Door was reorganised to accommodate the organ. The organ was purchased from Messrs Henry Willis & Son Ltd in 1924 and had originally been located in one of the side chapels. A new sanctuary tower was also constructed to complement Canon Foley's western tower (above the Great Western Door). The altar area was refurbished and three new stained-glass windows installed.

One of the most important shrines within the interior of the cathedral is the Shrine of Blessed Thaddeus McCarthy. Born in 1456, he was appointed Bishop of Ross on 29 March 1482 and was consecrated in Rome on 3 May. His bishopric was contested by Odo O'Driscoll, and McCarthy was subsequently denounced by Pope Innocent VII. He decided to travel to Rome to secure final confirmation that he was the rightful bishop. His business complete, he set out from Rome in July 1492 disguised as a pilgrim. He took ill on the journey, and died in a pilgrim hospital at Ivrea in Piedmont. Under the instruction of the Bishop of Ivrea, his remains were vested in Episcopal robes and buried in the cathedral church of Ivrea. Miracles were soon being attributed to him and in 1742 his body, which was said to be still intact, was removed to a new sarcophagus. To commemorate his life, a special ossuary containing his bones was placed on the right-hand side of the sanctuary in the cathedral. An oil painting depicting him as a pilgrim can be seen in the northern sanctuary.

ST MARY'S DOMINICAN CHURCH, POPE'S QUAY

Kearns Deane, brother of Sir Thomas Deane, was chosen to design St Mary's Dominican Church. He adopted a neo-classical design in accordance with the Grecian Ionic style of architecture. The church would resemble a Roman temple, with a portico of several pillars supporting an ornate pediment-style canopy. The selected stonemasons were Thomas & James Fitzgerald of the Grand Parade and they chose

A return to antiquity: Roman temple-style façade of St Mary's Dominican Church, Pope's Quay. The church was built between 1832 and 1839, but the façade was not added until the late nineteenth century.

limestone as the principal material. In November 1832, the foundation stone was laid and seven years later, on Sunday, 20 October 1839, the church was blessed for public worship by the Bishop of Cork, Most Rev. John Murphy DD. The most famous of the dignitaries present in the crowd that day was Daniel O'Connell.

The portico was not constructed until 1861. The fluted ionic columns are over ten metres high and are amongst the finest in Ireland. The statue of Our Lady that surmounts the portico was raised to its present position in December 1861. It is the work of James Cahill of Dublin and is a copy of a statue in the Piazza di Spagna, Rome.

The interior of the church is elegant and well-proportioned. The ceiling is supported by fluted columns of the Corinthian order and the coffered stuccowork was carried out by local craftsmen. The sanctuary is very impressive. Everything in it was designed by George Goldie: the high altar with its *reredos* (ornate panelling behind an altar) and *baldachino* (ornate porch-like structure over the altar), the sanctuary pavement, the choir stalls, the altar rails and gates and the pulpit. The present high altar is the third to have been erected since the opening of the church. The brass statues on either side of the tabernacle represent St Dominic and St Catherine, the marble statues on the *reredos* represent St Thomas Aquinas and St

Catherine. Above this is the emblem of the Sacred Heart. In July 1976 the altar was detached from the *reredos*, reinforced and brought forward.

The *baldachino* was erected in 1872. It comprises four splendid columns of polished red Aberdeen granite, nearly three metres high, sitting on pedestals of Sicilian white marble. Each of the pedestals has four panels of green Connemara marble. The columns are crowned by a large triangular pediment of Caen stone, at the base of which is inscribed a quote from the Book of Isaiah: *Vere Tu es Deus Absconditus,* or 'Truly you are a hidden God'. Around the sides of the pediment prayers are inscribed: *Ave, Maria, Gratia Plena,* or 'Hail Mary, full of grace', and *Ecce Ancilla Domini,* or 'Behold the hand-maid of the Lord'.

In 1871 a sanctuary lamp fashioned by Messrs John Smyth and Co., Dublin, was donated by the ladies of St Mary's Catechetical Society. A decorative pulpit is also located adjacent to the sanctuary. It is the work of Messrs PJ O'Neil and Sons, Dublin, and is composed of a variety of marbles: Carrara, Sicilian, Siena, Galway black and Midleton red. The figures represented are five Dominican saints: St Dominic (1170–1221), St Thomas Aquinas (1225–74), St Catherine of Siena (1347–80), St Pius V (1504–72) and St Vincent Ferrer (1350–1419). At the base are three niches housing figures representing *Faith, Hope* and *Charity.*

Within the altar rails are two side altars, the Altar of Our Lady of the Rosary and the Shrine of Our Lady of Graces. Both altars were designed by Samuel F Hynes and placed in position in 1889. The Altar of Our Lady of the Rosary is supported by eight granite columns with Corinthian capitals. A curved coning contains carved heads of Our Lady and St Joseph and of Mary's parents, St Joachim and St Anne. The Shrine of Our Lady of Graces is well known for its ivory image of Our Lady, an image reputed to have been brought to Youghal from Europe in 1304 by Maurice O'Carroll, Archbishop of Cashel. In the late eighteenth century, the Dominican order was compelled to abandon their church in Youghal due to the Penal Laws, and the relic was brought to Cork and encased in a larger shrine. It was placed in its present position in 1895.

Another altar is dedicated to St Dominic, the founder of the Dominican order, and above it in a recess is a statue of the saint. On the altar itself are four little carvings of head. They represent St

Dominic, St Thomas Aquinas, St Catherine of Siena and an unidentified female saint reputed to be St Rose of Lima. Beneath the slab of this altar are said to be the relics of an Early Christian martyr, St Severus. Outside the sanctuary, in the east and west transepts, are altars to the Sacred Heart and to St Joseph. Both were designed by George Goldie.

The large pipe organ at the back of the church was built and put in place by Messrs Conacher & Co., Dublin. Kneelers and dividing-rails were also put into place while the portico was being constructed. The first stations of the cross were supplied by Meyer & Co. of London in 1872. These stations comprised oil paintings in large wooden frames, but have since been lost. They were replaced in 1969 by the present stations of the cross, which are hand-carved and are the work of a wood-carving industry in Ortisei in the Dolomite Alps of Northern Italy.

The day the circus came to town: a parade of elephants and artists walks past Glanmire (now Kent) Station.

KENT STATION

Kent station, formerly Glanmire Station, is situated on the Lower Glanmire Road on the north side of the River Lee. It was the last of a series of five stations opened in the city in the late nineteenth century. It was originally built to replace the Dublin and Cobh stations, which were situated at Penrose Quay and Summerhill respectively. The deteriorating condition of those stations, along with an increase in the number of people using trains, meant that a new station had to be built. Thus in the early 1880s, it was proposed by the leading railway company in Cork City, the Great Southern and Western Railway, to build Kent Station. Today, it is the only railway terminus in Cork.

Building began in the late 1880s when the railway engine shed was built, followed by the coal gantry line. A goods warehouse already existed, but was turned around to face east instead of north and additional tracks were laid in the new goods yard. By 1890 the marshy land at the back of the houses on the Lower Glanmire Road had been filled in. In the spring of 1891 the real construction work began on the main station building. The contractor was a Mr Samuel Hill, who was a native of the city. The architecture chosen for the station was plain and functional, primarily comprising Ruabon brick faced with limestone. Two years later, in February 1893, the station opened to the public. The *Cork Constitution* reported that: 'Yesterday the new Cork Passenger terminus of the G. S. & W.R. was opened to traffic (at a final cost of £60,000) with the departure of the 6 a.m. train to Dublin. The last train had arrived in Summerhill around midnight, and at Penrose Quay at 2 a.m. and both these stations are now closed to regular traffic.'

The main building is approximately 100 metres long and has various retail outlets along with a booking area, which now houses an ornate steam engine, the Number 36 – the oldest engine on display in Ireland. Another covered building was constructed at a right angle to the main edifice in which there are two further platforms and an inclined subway. This area now also contains a railway museum, which includes a fabulous collection of rail-line insignia and a large mural by artist Marshall Hutson. The mural depicts an old Hibernia Locomotive on the first commuter line in the world, the Dublin–Kingstown (now Dún Laoghaire) line.

In the eastern wing of Kent Station two further platforms were constructed. From these platforms, trains ran to Cobh (Queenstown in those days) and Youghal; today, the trains run only to Cobh.

One of Kent Station's famous incidents occurred in the 1970s, when the name of the station was temporarily changed to Folkstone Harbour. This was due to the filming of *The Great Train Robbery*, starring Sean Connery and Lesley Anne Downes, which used the station for some scenes. The filmmakers chose Kent Station because the structure of the station had not changed since 1893, and therefore it was one of the few authentic Victorian railway stations remaining.

The opening of St Patrick's Bridge, as shown in the *Illustrated London News* on 14 December 1861.

ST PATRICK'S BRIDGE

As the butter trade in Cork grew in the late 1700s, there was a call for a new bridge to link the northside of the city with the customs houses and quaysides of the city centre (now the area of Emmet Place in front of Cork Opera House). The Corporation decided to take out a loan to finance the building of the new bridge. In order to facilitate repayment, it was further decided to place tolls on the proposed bridge for a period of twenty-one years. A Mr Michael Shanahan was chosen to be the architect and chief contractor of the operation. In 1788 he began drawing plans and on 25 July of that year, the foundation stone was laid. It took six months to complete the bridge.

Unfortunately, on Saturday, 17 January 1789 disaster struck when a flood swept through the Lee Valley. Contemporary newspaper accounts relate that from noon on Friday, 16 January to noon the following day, torrential rain caused wide-scale flooding that invaded all the flat ground in the city. During Saturday night, boats were seen

The original gas lights, erected in 1861, still
grace St Patrick's Bridge. There are
<u>eight lights in total.</u>

drifting down streets and laneways. It is said that the citizens held
out lights to warn incoming horse and carriages of the danger.

The following morning showed the full extent of the damage.
Numerous cabins had been swept away along with cattle, hay, corn
and furniture. The financial loss was estimated to be at least
£50,000. On Sunday morning, as the flood waters receded, the shattered centre arch of the nearly finished St Patrick's Bridge was discovered. An old boat moored at Carroll's Quay–Pope's Quay had
broken loose and crashed against the incomplete keystone of the
bridge, destroying it. The remaining arches had collapsed into the
waters of the raging Lee. The bridge had to be rebuilt and was finally
opened on 29 September 1789. Sometime after 1789 the Merchant's
Committee of Cork paid £1,400 for the right to collect tolls on the
bridge. A toll was charged until 1812, at which time the Committee
announced the tolls had paid off their losses from the rebuilding of
the bridge and abolished them.

In November 1853 disaster struck again when St Patrick's Bridge
was swept away by flood waters. This was due to a build-up of pressure
at North Gate Bridge, which was the only structure to remain

standing when the flood swept through the city, claiming several lives and destroying everything in its path. The Corporation applied to Westminster for permission to rebuild both St Patrick's Bridge and North Gate Bridge. Their applications were passed in 1856 and on 7 December 1853 a temporary timber structure, designed by Sir John Benson, was opened close to the damaged bridge to facilitate reconstruction.

In November 1859, the new St Patrick's Bridge opened. It comprised three arches over the river with an ornate pillared balustrade on both sides. The effigies on top of each arch were carved by Corkman PJ Scannell and depict St Patrick, St Bridget, *Neptune* and three sea-goddesses. Yet again the bridge had to be reconstructed after a small boat broke loose from its moorings and crashed into it. It was rebuilt and reopened on 12 December 1861. The bridge has not had to be rebuilt since, and it still spans the rushing waters of the River Lee. From the centre of the bridge, there is a beautiful view of the south channel and Gurranabraher.

SS. PETER AND PAUL'S CHURCH

For more than 100 years, SS. Peter and Paul's Church has stood in a quiet street off St Patrick's Street. The present building was opened on Friday, 29 June 1866 and replaced an older church that had fallen into disrepair. That church was built in 1786 and was called Carey's Lane Chapel. A portion of it was retained and used in the building of the present sacristy.

Plans for the present-day church were initially proposed in the 1820s. However, there was no one person to push the project along, and work never commenced. It was only on the arrival of Fr John Murphy to the parish that the project was revitalised under his direction. Entrusted with obtaining architectural plans for the rebuilding of the old chapel, Fr Murphy arranged a competition. In total, eight well-known architects submitted plans: EW Pugin, Hudfield, Murray, Atkins, Nicholls, Wigley, Hurley and Jones. Pugin was selected as the outright winner.

Work on the church got underway on 15 August 1859 when the foundation stone was laid. The new building was located just west of the old one due to space restrictions in the inner city, and this led to

Hidden from view, the elegant façade
of SS. Peter and Paul's Church displays
fine workmanship.

an immediate problem with space. To resolve the issue, Pugin modi-
fied some of his designs. The cost of the project was the next problem
for Fr John Murphy, who arranged many fundraising schemes to keep
the project going. His persistence paid off, and on Friday, 29 June
1866 the first Mass was said by Bishop Delany and the church was
dedicated to the Apostles Peter and Paul.

Pugin chose the Gothic style of architecture, the basic plan being
a nave with two side aisles. The material used was red sandstone with
dressings of limestone. The ridge of the roof of the church is decorated with ornamental ironwork, partly gilt, terminating at the western gable in an ornamental cross with foliated arms. The western
doorway is the main entrance. It is recessed and the jambs are ornamented. A triangular heading surmounts the arch over the doorway
and the doors are hung with ornamental iron hinges of the most skil-
ful and beautiful workmanship, while on either side small blank
arches in the manner of an arcade flank the principal doorway. Over
the doorway is the Great Western Window, the upper portion of
which is occupied with geometrical tracery and ornamental pillars.

From the top of the window to the roof, narrow horizontal bands of limestone break the monotony of the gable end.

The nave terminates in an apse (altar area) of polygonal form, lit by eight narrow windows, four of which have side pillars decorated with heads. The aisles are divided from the nave by an arcade of eight arches, four on each side. The clerestory lights the nave and its large windows have ornate pillars on either side. The roof is of open timberwork, the principal beams resting on corbels that are carved with various angelic figures.

There are five columns on either side of the nave forming eight arches. The bases of these columns are black marble. The plinths and columns are polished red marble, while the capitals are carved with fruit and flowers. The red marble had previously been used to mend roads, but after its use in this church it was deemed a most beautiful and valuable marble and hundreds of tonnes of it were exported to England for the adornment of public buildings. The other pillars in the church, around the side altars, are carved in white Sicilian marble and Galway green marble, while under the choir more red marble is visible, quarried in Little Island, County Cork.

The three altars – the grand altar and two side altars – are objects of great beauty and interest. It was a number of years after the opening of the church that the grand altar was supplied. Prior to that, a temporary altar had been used, which the *Cork Daily Reporter* described as 'carefully decorated and handsomely constructed'. It was decorated in pure white and gold, representing purity and charity. It was proposed in 1866 that the permanent grand altar be built entirely of the purest white Carrara statuary marble.

The dome of the apse is a marvel of artistry. Against a blue background its golden decorations are dazzling. They consist chiefly of the various emblematic figures of the keys and swords of SS. Peter and Paul, a pelican, cherubim and seraphim. The seven handsome lamps hanging before the altar represent the seven spirits standing before the throne of the angels of the ancient Church, referring to the seven churches of Asia. Up in the clerestory are two fine statues of SS. Peter and Paul, one on either side; the first was presented by JF Maguire MP, the other by Sir William Hackett. Beside these are two panels representing St Peter delivered out of prison by the angels and the epiphany of St Paul on the road to Damascus.

The steps up to the grand altar and the pavements surrounding the altar are all of white Italian veined marble. The entire flooring of the church consists of alternate pieces of white and black marble, representing the Church of God that welcomes saints and sinners alike. At the extremities, near the pews, the black-and-white marble flooring is bordered by a flesh-coloured marble. This represents the temptations of the body in the physical world. In 1866 the baptistry was located, as in all churches of the time, at the southwestern angle of the building. A spiral stone staircase leads up to it and the choir area, which lies beneath the Great Western Window, and is supported by a colonnade of double marble pillars forming three archways. Pugin's timeless design still looks elegant and impressive to this day.

CHRIST CHURCH
AND ST PETER'S CHURCH

In 1608, according to the charter of James I, the medieval walled town of Cork contained just two parishes. Christ Church was located on the marshy island adjacent to South Main Street, whilst St Peter's overlooked North Main Street. In each parish, there was a basic stone church and a municipal graveyard. These two churches were

The impressive exterior of the medieval Christ Church, which now houses the Cork Archive Institute.

One of only two churches within the walled town of Cork, St Peter's Church (shown here prior to renovation) now houses the Cork Vision Centre.

Christian until the Reformation, at which time they were given to the Protestant community. Both are still standing today but are quite different in form and function from their medieval counterparts.

It is thought that the history of **Christ Church** extends back at least 1,000 years. The first church on the site was probably constructed by the Danish Vikings c.AD1,000. When the Anglo-Normans seized control of the Viking town of Cork in 1177, they built their Christ Church on the same site. The Anglo-Norman church comprised a tower, a steeple and a belfry. Within the church precinct was a college, or a basic schoolhouse, an almshouse, gardens, graveyard and houses for the priests. In the course of time, more features were added to the church complex, such as a crypt, a chapel in praise of the Crusades, a hostel and an organ taken from a Spanish galleon by Sir Francis Drake, which he donated c.1588.

The graveyard was the burial place of the city's wealthy merchants and mayors. One tomb still on display is that of Thomas Ronan, Mayor of Cork in 1537 and 1549. It is known as the Modest Man, referring to Ronan's humble devotion to God. Originally placed in the crypt, the stone slab depicts a shroud tied at the top and bottom, with an opening in the middle displaying a skeletal figure. Above the shroud are the sun and moon, below a star and a rose, along with the letters T.R. The signs of the Four Evangelists occupy the four corners of the slab, though one is now missing. The accompanying inscription tells of the interring of Thomas Ronan in 1554 and of his wife, Johanna Tirry, in 1569, which warns the reader: *Be mindful O Man, since death tarries not, for whom thou diest, thou shalt inherit serpents, beasts and worms.*

During the turbulent Irish rebel days of the sixteenth century, Christ Church, also known as Holy Trinity, was chosen by the Protestant Corporation of Cork as their official church. During the Siege of Cork in 1690, Irish rebels captured some of the Protestant inhabitants and locked them in the towers of Christ Church, St Peter's Church and Queen's Castle. Unfortunately, Christ Church was badly damaged by a cannon ball in the siege, which crashed into the roof and destroyed it.

The third Christ Church was built between 1719 and 1720 and was designed by George Coltsman, who also redesigned the jailhouses at South and North Gate Bridges. This church was similar to previous structures, with a prominent tower at its western end. An unforeseen problem arose when the foundations of the tower subsided, causing the tower to lean to one side like the tower of Pisa, although not as dramatically. Over the years, various renovations were carried out to correct the tower's position, but they were not successful and the 'leaning tower' can still be seen today.

St Peter's Church is the second church to be built on the site overlooking North Main Street. Reference to the first church is made in Pope Innocent III's *Decretal Letter*, which states that the first church was built here in 1199. It would have been a large stone building with a tall tower. The building is best described in Charles Smith's *History of Cork* (1750):

> 'This is now the oldest church standing in the city. The steeple is detached a considerable way to the west of the church, and served as a tower to defend the city wall. This church is about 90 feet long but not of proportionable breadth; it has a tolerable neat altar-piece consisting of fluted Corinthian pilasters. Over the communion table is a dove painted, surrounded in glory in a pediment. On the west is a

mayor's gallery, over which are the King's arms,
carved and painted; and on each side are parallel
galleries and double rows of pews.'

Smith also described a graveyard belonging to the church, which
he noted dated to the 1500s. An unfortunate incident at this graveyard was recorded by Francis Tuckey in *Cork Remembrancer* (1837):
'One Francis Taylor was buried in St Peter's Church-yard, and the
next morning was found sitting up in the grave, one of his shoulders
much mangled, one of his hands full of clay, and blood running from
his eyes, a melancholy instance of the fatal consequences of a too pre-
cipitate interment.'

In 1782 this church was taken down and in 1783 building commenced on the present limestone-walled church. It has a similar
design to the original building, also based on a rectangular plan, and
was completed in 1788. At a later stage, a new tower was added but
had to be taken down again because it had been built on marshy, soft
ground. The weight of the tower while it was *in situ* had caused the
west-facing wall to tilt and sink slightly. As a result, many repairs and
alterations were carried out on St Peter's Church from the late 1700s
on to reinforce the structure.

In 1949 St Peter's Church of Ireland was deconsecrated. From
then until 1994, the church was used as a storehouse and was sadly
neglected. In 1994 the Cork Historic Centre Action Plan funded
extensive renovations of the church and reopened it as the Cork
Vision Centre, an exhibition centre that displays the past, present
and future development plans of the city. On display also is an elaborate model of the city centre. One of the most interesting monu-
ments in the Centre is the Deane monument. Dedicated to the
memory of Sir Matthew Deane, a sculpted effigy shows Deane on the
side of an altar tomb in an attitude of solemn prayer. It is inscribed:
Sr. Matthew Deane, Baronet, 1710. The family's coat of arms can also
be seen in the Cork Vision Centre.

BANKING INSTITUTIONS

Two fine nineteenth-century buildings stand near Cork's City Hall –
one is the former Cork Provincial Bank located at the entrance to the
South Mall and to Parnell Place, and now the property of Thomas

The Cork Provincial Bank, which was in operation until recent years. The building is now owned by Thomas Crosbie Holdings and is awaiting redevelopment.

Crosbie Holdings, the second is the Trustee Savings Bank (TSB),
which dominates Lapp's Quay and Parnell Place. It was in the early
eighteenth century that financial houses became prominent in Ireland. The earliest bank in the city was established c.1675 by Edward
and Joseph Hoare, wine merchants, and prospered in the early
1700s. It was located in a medieval laneway called Hoare's Lane,
which runs at a right angle to North Main Street. This laneway and
the buildings of Hoare's Bank were destroyed in the late 1820s to
create Adelaide Street.

On 2 December 1817 a select committee of Cork's wealthy merchants began discussing the idea of setting up a savings bank. The
meeting took place in the Commercial Buildings on the South Mall,
now the Imperial Hotel, and was organised by the Catholic Bishop, Dr
John Murphy. The Protestant bishop, Dr Thomas St Lawrence,
chaired the meeting. The idea was proposed by Dr. Murphy, supported by William Beamish, and was seconded by thirty trustees.
Within two weeks, the bank opened for business at the Royal Cork
Institution for two hours per week with two members of staff.

The building that still operates as the TSB was built in a neo-
classical style. The stone used in its construction came from a limestone quarry in Beaumont (now defunct), in the southern suburbs of

the city. The exterior ground-floor walls are faced with ashlar. The superstructure is supported by Ionic columns, four on each side. Those on the Parnell Place side are flanked by projecting pilaster wings crowned with pediments. The entrance vestibule is sombre and provides a fitting approach to the Banking Hall.

The interior is similar to that of St Mary's Dominican Church, Pope's Quay. All the fittings are executed in Spanish mahogany, which has mellowed over the years to a beautiful rich tone. The ceiling, cornices and doorways are coffered and richly covered with delicate ornamentations in the Greek Revival style. One of the special art treasures once housed here was a large sculpture of William Crawford by early nineteenth-century Cork artist John Hogan. Crawford had been one of several chartered proprietors of the Royal Cork Institution. Friends and admirers subscribed to this memorial. Once completed, the patrons realised there was no public building suitable to house it. The trustees of the bank invited them to erect it in the banking hall. There it remained until the 1970s when it was placed in the Sculpture Gallery of the Crawford Municipal Art Gallery, where it still stands.

Located on the corner of the South Mall and Parnell Place, overlooking Parnell Bridge, the Cork Provincial Bank was built between 1863 and 1865 and was acclaimed by many as the 'handsomest' public building in Cork. Costing between £15,000 and £20,000, it complemented the older TSB building opposite on Lapp's Quay. Built of white limestone, it was designed by Alexander Deane, an uncle of Sir Thomas Deane, with William J Murray as architect. The ornate style is described as High Victorian Classicism.

The exterior walls are faced with ashlar limestone. The ground-floor windows have semicircular heads and there are two large niches on either side of the main entrance. No statues have ever been placed in them. On the exterior of the second and upper storeys fluted Corinthian columns divide the space and support a large pediment in front and two smaller ones on the sides. Semicircular arches over the first-floor windows bear the coats of arms of Athlone, Derry, Galway, Cork, Wexford and Waterford. Irish Provincial Bank emblems are also represented here. Over the windows in the Parnell Place frontage are the coats of arms of Sligo, Belfast, Cork, Dublin and Ireland; all of these towns had provincial banks. On the main frontage, which projects out from the building, there are more semicircular arches bearing carved symbols of commerce, industry, agriculture and shipping. In addition, the bank monograms, or seals, are carved on the main elevation, and a sculpted head of Queen Victoria is carved on the keystone on the main façade.

The ceiling inside is domed and coffered and trimmed with deeply incised plasterwork. Floral and agricultural motifs are inscribed on a bracketed cornice. Pendant tracery breaks into symmetrical patterns and reforms into a wide marble floor with a frieze. The corridors are lined with limestone and the panelled offices have arched, deep-set windows, marble fireplaces and ornate spiral staircases. The main staircase is impressive with elaborate hanging newel posts and banisters carved as shamrocks. Beneath street level there are barrel-roofed strong rooms and subterranean vaults. The former Provincial Bank has recently been sold by Allied Irish Banks to Thomas Crosbie Holdings, whose intention is to convert it for offices. The Cork Provincial Bank remains one of the finest and most beautiful buildings in the city.

THE COURTHOUSE

Prior to 1835 two courthouses – a city and a county courthouse – administered the city. With an absence of historical records, all that is known of the County Courthouse is that it was built sometime in the early eighteenth century and stood on the site of the old Queen's Castle. The main building of the old City Courthouse, constructed in the early eighteenth century, stood on the site of Shandon Castle on the north side of the city, near the site of what is now the Firkin Crane Dance Centre.

In 1829 Cork Corporation decided that both of the courthouses should be merged into one building. A site on Washington Street was appointed. A competition for the design of the new City Courthouse was held and was won by the Pain brothers. They proposed a Corinthian design, or in essence a Roman temple design, which was similar to two other edifices in the city at the time: the Deanes's St Mary's Dominican Church, Pope's Quay, and the Pains's St Patrick's Church. At one stage during the construction of the building, the Deanes became the contractors for the courthouse. Still smarting from losing the contract to the Pains, it is said that Thomas Deane

The courthouse in 2003, post-renovations. It first opened in 1835
and is built of dressed limestone.

paid a stonemason £5 to remove the Pain name from the building.
Perhaps it's an urban legend, but it would certainly explain why the
name Pain does not feature on any of the stones.

Finished in 1835, the building is elegant and well-proportioned. The
front of the building, facing onto Washington Street, has a noble Corinthian portico. The front range of columns project out nearly six metres
from the building. The pillars are nearly ten metres high and are
approached by eleven steps, which rise almost two metres above the
present street level. The portico measures twenty metres in width. The
group of figures that stood over the original building represented *Justice, Law* and *Mercy*.

Inside, a marble central hall is overlooked by a great dome and pillared balcony. There are two semicircular courts, behind which lie the
public offices. The roof comprises beamed arches. Ornate balustrades
and panelling along with antique furniture and fittings lend an ageless
feel to the place.

On Good Friday, 27 March 1891 the interior was completely
destroyed by fire. The fire began in the eastern section of the building
and rapidly spread to engulf the entire structure. Fortunately, the

magnificent Corinthian portico survived. Allegedly, the fire was linked to events in the courts in the days prior to the blaze. Rioting had taken place in Tipperary and five men were arrested and their case was heard at the Cork City Courthouse. During the trial, the accused were jailed in the Courthouse and had to be rescued by court officials when the fire broke out. It is not known how the fire started; a full enquiry was carried out but no definite answers were found. The fire destroyed many of the municipal records of Cork.

In the following weeks, while the rebuilding work was carried out, court sessions were heard at the Model School on Anglesea Street (now the District Courthouse). Designs for a new Courthouse on the same site were again invited. Cork Corporation received thirteen submissions, and one was selected. The chosen designer was William Henry Hill. He retained the portico and reconstructed the interior in a style sympathetic to the original, recreating many features, such as the beamed arched roof and ornate balustrades.

Work commenced in July of that year and it was hoped that the building would be opened again after twenty-one months. The period of the project went far beyond the estimated time of completion, mainly due to trade strikes and bad weather. Thirty-three months later, on 18 March 1895, the first rooms of the new and present Courthouse were opened for the Spring Assizes. In April of that year, Hill finally finished his work and in September the building was officially opened by Lord Lieutenant of Ireland Earl Cadogan.

In the mid-twentieth century the railings surrounding the building were removed and the interior of the Courthouse was modernised, and the exterior walls were renovated. There are now four principal court rooms. The building is still elegant and beautifully proportioned and one is reminded of John Windele's description of it in *History of Cork* (1844) as 'decidedly the finest structure in the South of Ireland'.

ROYAL CORK INSTITUTION AND THE CANOVA CASTS

Based on institutions such as the Royal Society of London and the Royal Dublin Society, the Royal Cork Institution (RCI) was founded in 1803 by Rev. Thomas Dix Hincks, minister of the Old Presbyterian Church in Princes Street. He aimed to create a 'useful and honourable' institution in the city, covering the areas of languages,

Two of the famous Canova casts that reside in
the Crawford Municipal Art Gallery.

literature, logic, elementary mathematics, natural history and
experimental sciences.

In 1807 the institution was incorporated and renamed the Royal
Cork Institution. From small beginnings at premises on the South
Mall, opposite the Imperial Hotel, the RCI operated as a British
State-supported research and teaching centre for over seventy years.
The Institution tailored its courses to the interests of its members;
no certificates or qualifications were offered. As well as courses,
there were public lectures on science and the application of scientific principles to industry and agriculture. There were also demon-
strations in chemistry, electricity, botany and mineralogy. In
essence, the Institution pioneered the concept of adult education
albeit for wealthy adults only.

In 1823 the full catalogue of the Institution's library consisted of
5,000–6,000 volumes, along with a large private and public patents
collection. (A copy of this catalogue can be viewed in the Boole

Library, UCC.) The books held in the library covered a broad spec-
trum: agriculture, natural history, chemistry, natural philosophy,
medicine, history and philology (the scientific study of the origin and
development of language).

One of the RCI's most important acquisitions was a collection of
casts of classical sculptures. These contributed hugely to the early
artistic training of two of Ireland's foremost nineteenth-century artists: painter Daniel Maclise (1800–58) and sculptor John Hogan
(1806–70). The story behind the acquisition of these casts is
interesting. Anxious to express his gratitude to the English people
for the return to the Vatican Galleries of many of the masterpieces
looted by Napoleon, Pope Pius VII commissioned Antonio Canova
(1755–1822) to make a set of over 200 plaster casts of famous
Roman and Greek sculptures held in the Vatican, including the
Discus Thrower and the magnificent *Laocoön* masterpiece. In 1822,
they were shipped to London as a gift to the Prince Regent, later
George IV. The prince did not care for the gift and the casts lay first

A cast by Canova of one of the most magnificent treasures owned by the Vatican – *Laocoön and His Sons*,
originally sculpted by Athanadoros, Hagesandros and
Polydoros of Rhodes in the early first century.

in the London Custom House and then in the basement of his residence in Carleton Gardens. Lord Listowel of Convamore, County
Cork, a patron of the arts and a friend of the prince, suggested that
the casts be donated to the people of Cork. The prince agreed and
presented them to the Society of Fine Arts in 1818, whose premises
was located on the intersection of St Patrick Street and Falkener's
Lane.

An account by Daniel Maclise describes how a former theatre on St
Patrick's Street, once used by the Apollo Society of Amateur Actors,
was chosen as the most suitable place for storing the valuable collection. However, shortly after receiving them, the Society of Fine Arts
found itself unable to pay the rent on the premises, and with considerable embarrassment applied to the government for financial aid.
No grant was awarded, but the government recommended that the
Society join forces with the RCI and pool their resources. They did so,
and an arrangement was made whereby the RCI paid the sum owed by
the Society of Fine Arts and, in return, the casts became the property
of the RCI. Maclise recounted that the collection was subsequently
removed to a sculpture gallery at the Cork Institution, now the Crawford Municipal Art Gallery.

By the 1820s financial problems were threatening the future of the
Institution. It requested that its finances be examined by the Commission on Education in Ireland, which examined the use made of public
grants in the area of elementary education. After conducting an investigation, the Commissioners recommended that the Institution's
six-acre botanic garden be disposed of in order to cut down on expen-
diture. Subsequently, on 31 December 1826, Henry Goulburn of the
Commissioners of Inquiry sent a letter to the institution stating that
their grant would be reduced to £1,500 and that agricultural activities
must be curtailed. In 1828, Westminster withdrew its financial support of the RCI. To compensate for this, the city gave the eighteenth-
century custom house on Emmet Place to the RCI.

In the 1830s the RCI influenced the government in its decision to
establish a university not only in Cork but in Galway and Belfast, too.
It also established the Crawford Art and Design School, now Cork
Institute of Technology (CIT). By 1850 inadequate funds and lack of
public support led to the RCI being reconstituted as a private society.
The activities of the Royal Cork Institution eventually ceased c.1885.